ESSENTIAL ELEMENTS for Band

COMPREHENSIVE BAND METHOD

TIM LAUTZENHEISER • JOHN HIGGINS • CHARLES MENGHINI
PAUL LAVENDER • TOM C. RHODES • DON BIERSCHENK

To create an account, visit:
www.essentialelementsinteractive.com

Student Activation Code
E2AS-0905-0700-9042

ISBN 979-835013677-7

REVIEW
KEY SIGNATURE
Key of G
TIME SIGNATURES
BREATH MARK
F♯
G
A
B
C
D
E
REPEAT SIGN
TIE
SLUR
TEMPO MARKINGS
Allegro
Moderato
NOTES
RESTS
Whole
Half
Quarter
Eighths
1. TECHNIQUE TRAX
2. WELCOME SONG
African Folk Song
Allegro
mf
3. THAILAND LULLABY
Thai Folk Song
Moderato
4. SHEPHERD'S HEY
English Folk Song
Moderato
5. THE CRAWDAD SONG
American Folk Song
Allegro

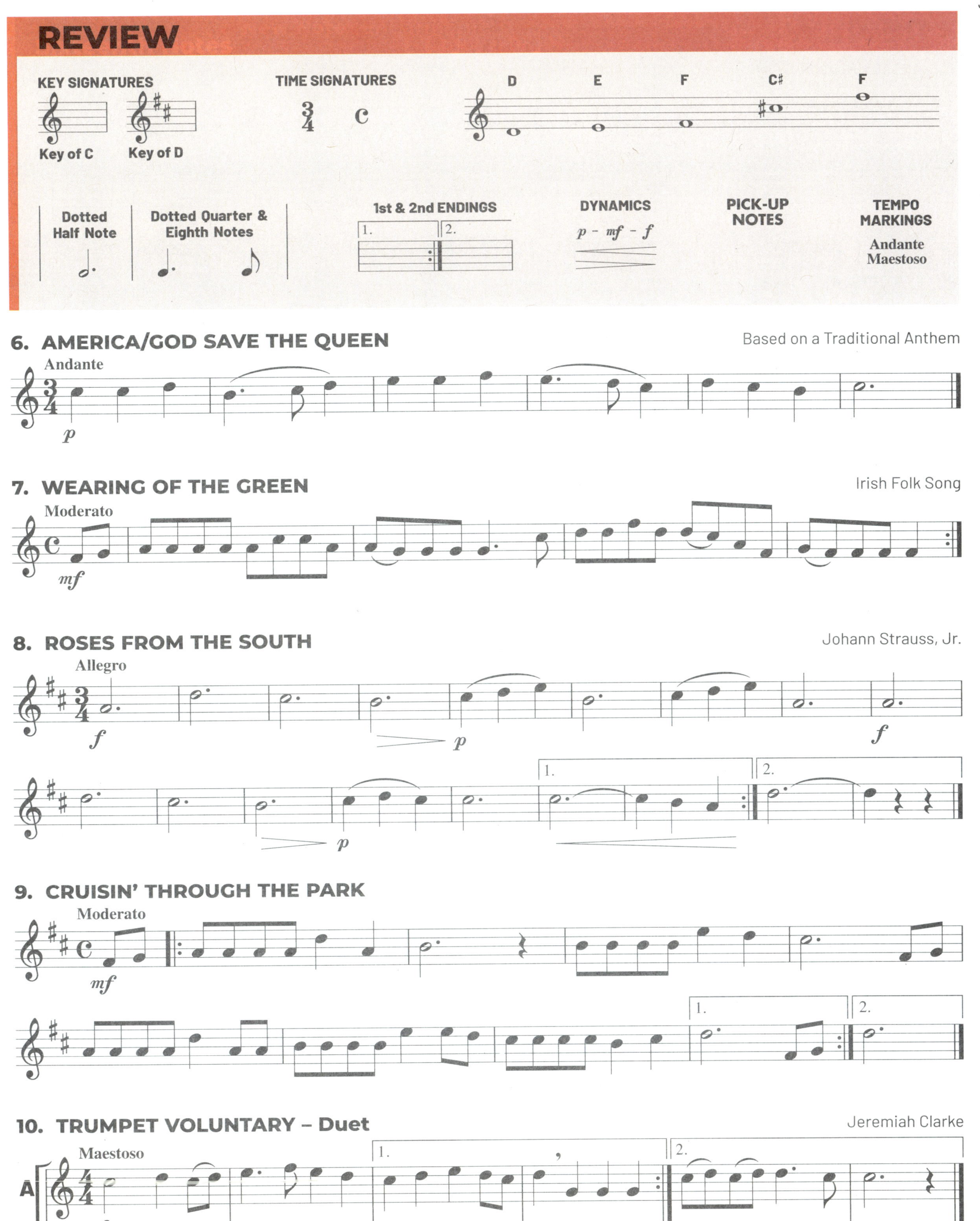
REVIEW
KEY SIGNATURES
Key of C
Key of D
TIME SIGNATURES
D
E
F
C♯
F
Dotted Half Note
Dotted Quarter & Eighth Notes
1st & 2nd ENDINGS
1.
2.
DYNAMICS
p - mf - f
PICK-UP NOTES
TEMPO MARKINGS
Andante
Maestoso
6. AMERICA/GOD SAVE THE QUEEN
Based on a Traditional Anthem
Andante
p
7. WEARING OF THE GREEN
Irish Folk Song
Moderato
mf
8. ROSES FROM THE SOUTH
Johann Strauss, Jr.
Allegro
f
p
f
1.
2.
p
9. CRUISIN' THROUGH THE PARK
Moderato
mf
1.
2.
10. TRUMPET VOLUNTARY – Duet
Jeremiah Clarke
Maestoso
1.
2.
A
B
f
f

REVIEW
MULTIPLE MEASURE REST
2
ACCENT
FERMATA
D.C. al FINE
F♯
G
A
Eighth Note & Eighth Rest
Eighth Rest & Eighth Note
Eighth Note & Dotted Quarter Note
ENHARMONICS
A♯
B♭
D♯
E♭
11. CHROMA-ZONE
mf
Alt. F♯
Alt.
Fine
2
D.C. al Fine
f
12. BILLY BOY
American Folk Song
Moderato
f
mf
13. TECHNIQUE TRAX
Allegro
f
1.
2.
14. SALSA SIESTA – Duet
Moderato
A
B
f
p
mf

Staccato

Staccato notes are played lightly and with separation. They are marked with a dot above or below the note.

15. TREADING LIGHTLY

Tenuto

Tenuto notes are played smoothly and connected, holding each note until the next is played. They are marked with a straight line above or below the note.

16. SMOOTH MOVE

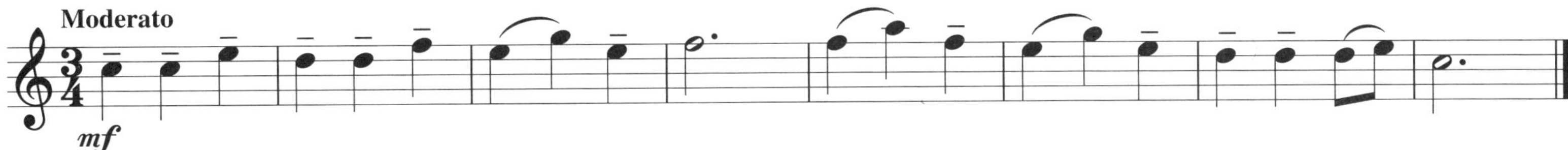

17. SHIFTING GEARS

HISTORY

English composer **Thomas Tallis** (1508–1585) served as a royal court composer for Kings Henry VIII and Edward VI, and Queens Mary and Elizabeth. During Tallis' lifetime, the artist Michelangelo painted the Sistine Chapel.

Canons (one or more parts imitating the first part) were used in many forms by 16th century composers. A **Round** is a strict (or exact) canon which can be repeated any number of times without stopping. Play *Tallis Canon* as a 4-part round.

18. TALLIS CANON (Round)

Thomas Tallis

Sightreading

Sightreading means playing a musical piece for the first time. The key to sightreading success is to know what to look for *before* you play. Use the word **S-T-A-R-S** to remind yourself what to look for, and eventually your band will become sightreading STARS!

- **S** – **Sharps or flats** in the key signature
- **T** – **Time signature** and **tempo markings**
- **A** – **Accidentals** not found in the key signature
- **R** – **Rhythms**, silently counting the more difficult notes and rests
- **S** – **Signs**, including dynamics, articulations, repeats and endings

19. SIGHTREADING CHALLENGE

DAILY WARM-UPS

WORK-OUTS FOR TONE & TECHNIQUE

20. TONE BUILDER

21. FLEXIBILITY STUDY

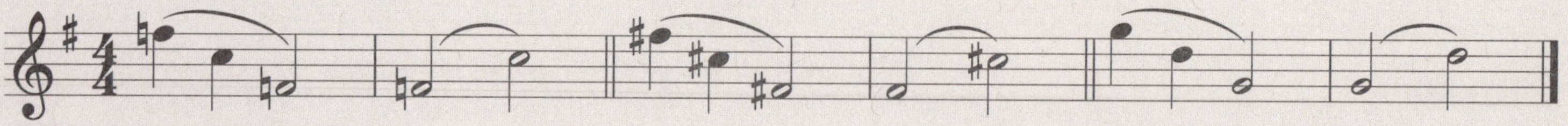

22. TECHNIQUE TRAX

23. CHORALE

Johann Sebastian Bach

Andante

p

mf

p

24. GRANDFATHER'S CLOCK

Henry C. Work

Ritardando *ritard.* (or) *rit.* – Gradually slower.

25. GLOW WORM

Paul Lincke

26. ALMA MATER – New Note *Practice long tones on all new notes.*

A.C. Weekes, W.M. Smith, H.S. Thompson

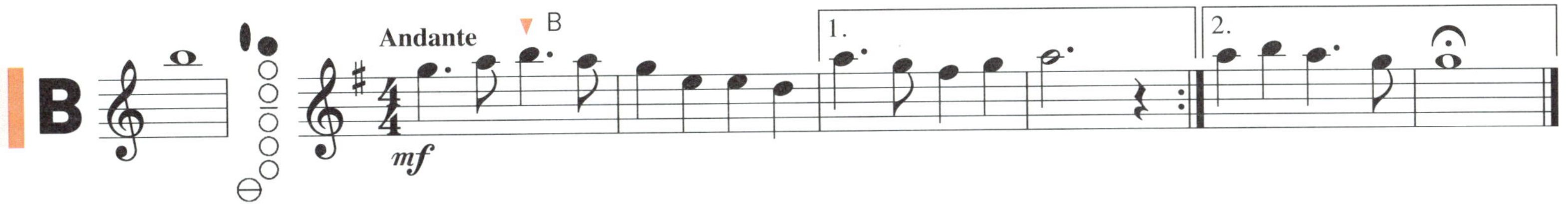

HISTORY

The Scottish folk song *Loch Lomond* is credited to an anonymous soldier who was imprisoned and awaiting execution. In it he writes of his desire to return home to his family and the breathtaking beauty of Loch (Lake) Lomond, a lake in Scotland. Located in the southern highlands, the lake is almost entirely surrounded by hills. One of these is Ben Lomond, a peak 3,192 feet high.

27. LOCH LOMOND

Scottish Folk Song

THEORY

Key Changes

If a key signature changes during a piece of music, you will usually see a thin double bar line at the **key change**. You may also see natural signs reminding you to "cancel" previous sharps or flats. Keep playing, using the correct notes indicated in the *new* key signature.

28. MOLLY MALONE

Irish Folk Song

Dynamics

cresc. = *crescendo* (or)

decresc. = *decrescendo* (or)

29. RISE AND FALL

30. NO COMPARISON

31. SIGHTREADING CHALLENGE *Remember the S-T-A-R-S guidelines.*

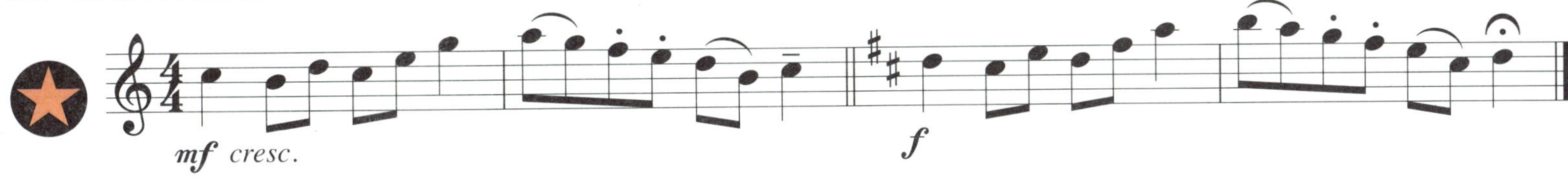

THEORY
¢ Time Signature
Cut Time (Alla Breve)
or
= 2 beats per measure
= Half note gets one beat
= 2 beats
= 1 beat
= ½ beat
32. RHYTHM RAP Clap the rhythm while counting and tapping.
Clap
1 & 2 &
33. A CUT ABOVE
34. TWO-FOUR YANKEE DOODLE
American Folk Song
Moderato
mf
35. CUT TIME YANKEE DOODLE
American Folk Song
Moderato
mf
36. MARIANNE
Jamaican Folk Song
Moderato
p cresc.
f decresc.
1.
2.
p
37. THE VICTORS
Louis Elbel
March Tempo
f
Count ► 1 & 2 &
1.
2.
1 & 2 &
38. ESSENTIAL CREATIVITY Write this example in cut time ¢ before playing.
Allegro
f
Allegro

Dynamics

mp — *mezzo piano* (moderately soft)

Use full breath support at all dynamic levels.
p – *mp* – *mf* – *f*

39. A - ROVING

Syncopation

Syncopation occurs when an accent or emphasis is given to a note that is not on a strong beat. This type of "off-beat" feel is common in many popular and classical styles.

THEORY

40. RHYTHM RAP

41. IN SYNC

42. LA ROCA

Puerto Rican Folk Song

American composer **George M. Cohan** (1878–1942) was also a popular author, producer, director and performer. He helped develop a popular form of American musical theater now known as musical comedy. He is also considered to be one of the most famous composers of American patriotic songs, earning the Congressional Medal of Honor in 1917 for his song *Over There*. Many of his songs became morale boosters when the United States entered World War I in that same year.

HISTORY

43. ESSENTIAL ELEMENTS QUIZ – YOU'RE A GRAND OLD FLAG

Words and Music by George M. Cohan

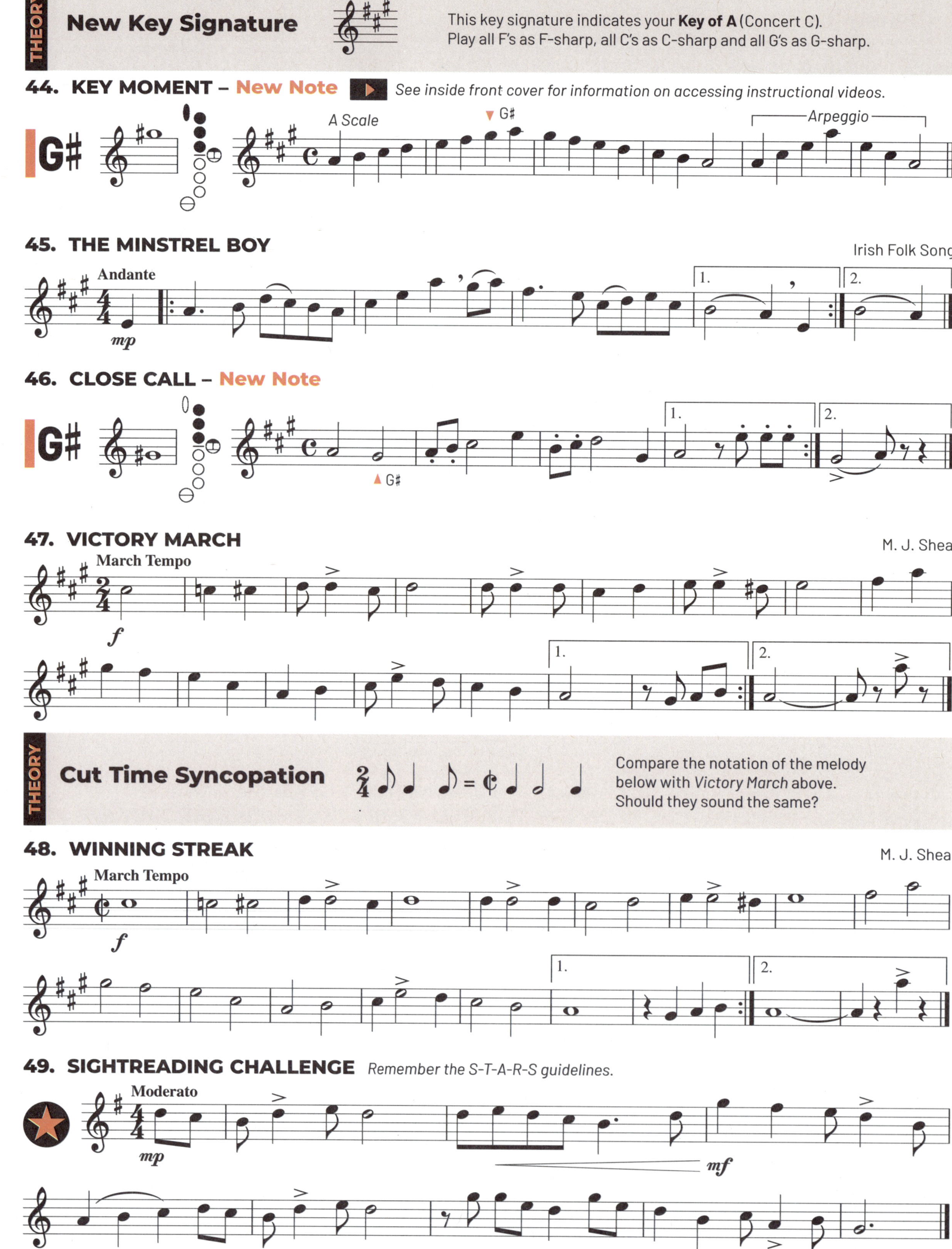
THEORY
New Key Signature
This key signature indicates your **Key of A** (Concert C).
Play all F's as F-sharp, all C's as C-sharp and all G's as G-sharp.
44. KEY MOMENT – New Note
See inside front cover for information on accessing instructional videos.
G♯
A Scale
G♯
Arpeggio
45. THE MINSTREL BOY
Irish Folk Song
Andante
mp
1.
2.
46. CLOSE CALL – New Note
G♯
G♯
1.
2.
47. VICTORY MARCH
M. J. Shea
March Tempo
f
1.
2.
THEORY
Cut Time Syncopation
Compare the notation of the melody below with *Victory March* above. Should they sound the same?
48. WINNING STREAK
M. J. Shea
March Tempo
f
1.
2.
49. SIGHTREADING CHALLENGE
Remember the S-T-A-R-S guidelines.
Moderato
mp
mf
mp

4 sixteenth notes = 1 Beat
Each sixteenth note = ¼ Beat

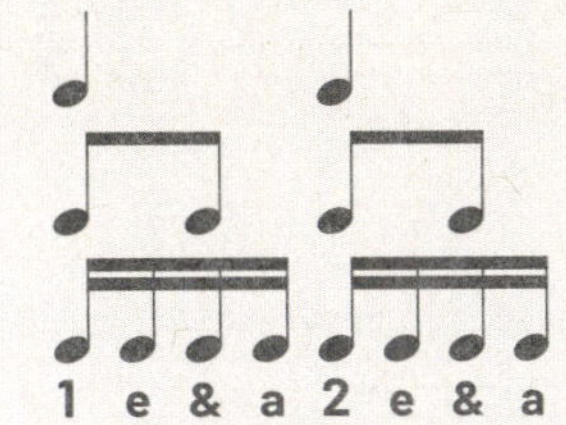

A single sixteenth note has 2 flags on the stem.

50. RHYTHM RAP

51. SIXTEENTH NOTE FANFARE

52. MOVING ALONG

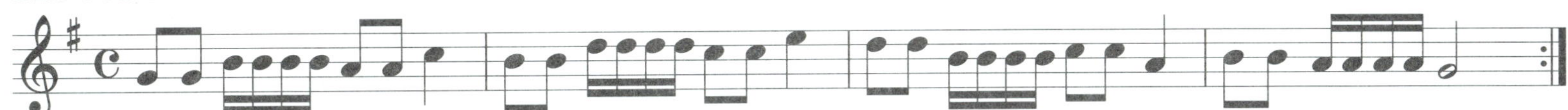

53. BACK AND FORTH – Duet

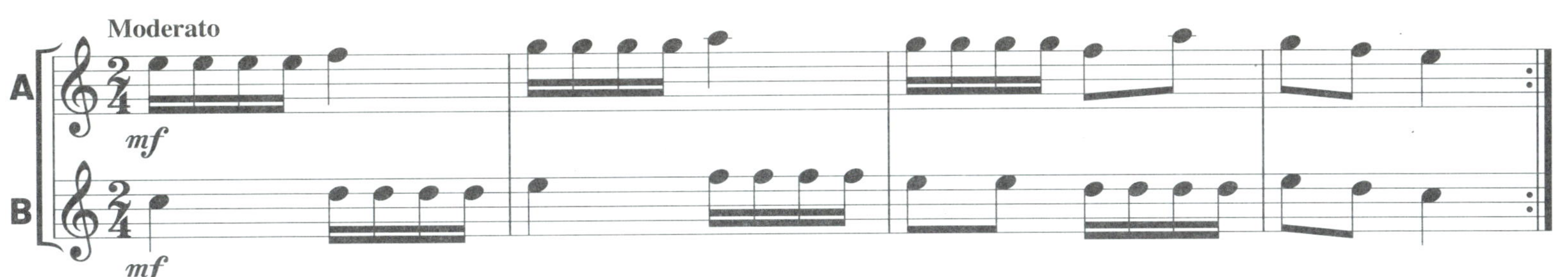

54. COMIN' ROUND THE MOUNTAIN VARIATIONS

55. ESSENTIAL ELEMENTS QUIZ

PERFORMANCE SPOTLIGHT

PERFORMANCE SPOTLIGHT

60. LAS MAÑANITAS – Band Arrangement

Mexican Folk Song
Arr. by John Higgins

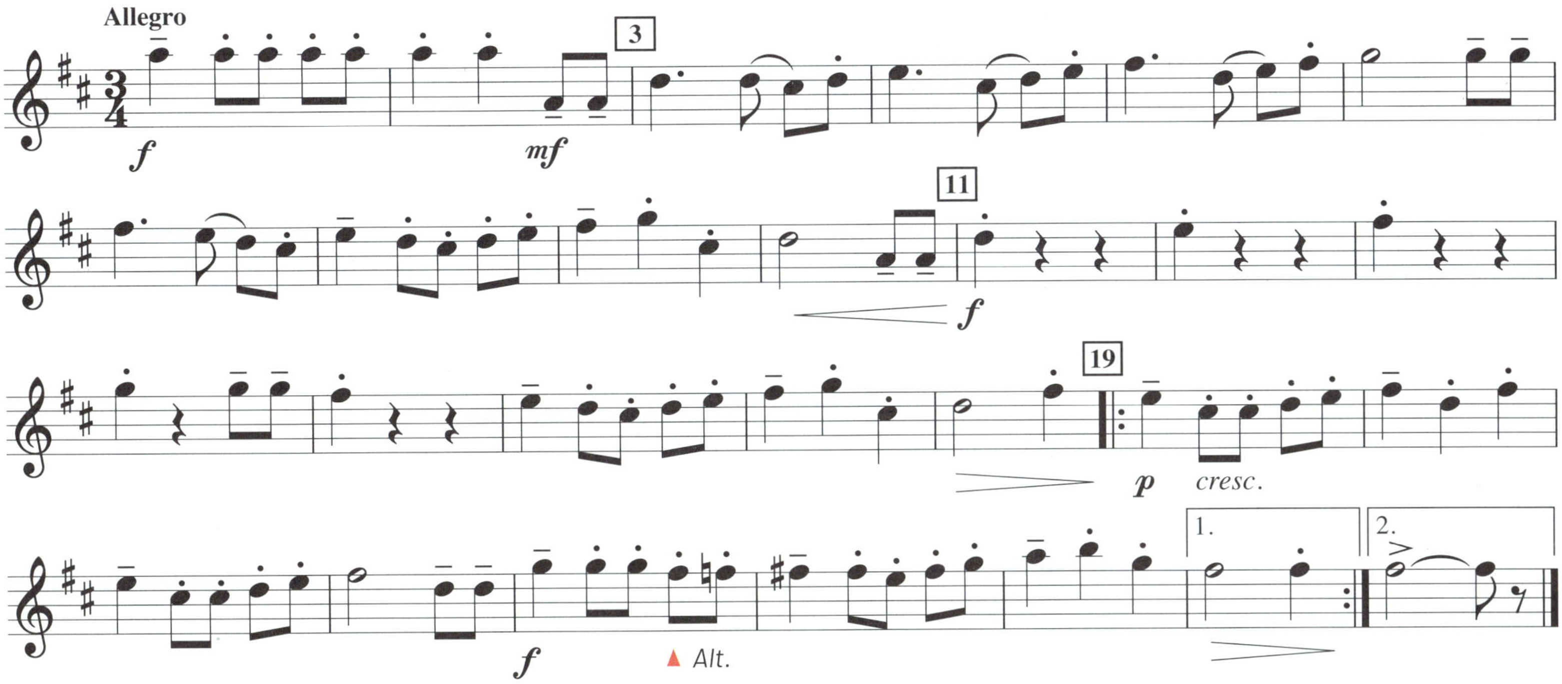

Allegro

f mf f p *cresc.* f ▲ Alt.

61. RONDEAU – Band Arrangement

Jean-Joseph Mouret
Arr. by John Higgins

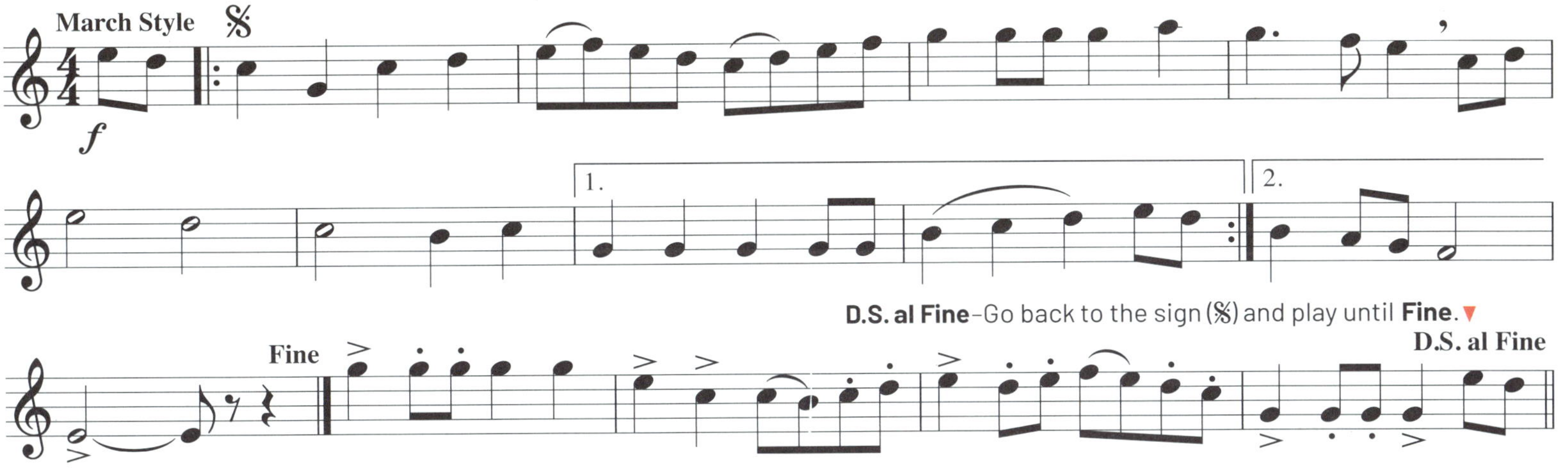

March Style

f

D.S. al Fine–Go back to the sign (𝄋) and play until **Fine**.▼

Fine

D.S. al Fine

62. ROCK.COM – Encore Band Arrangement

John Higgins

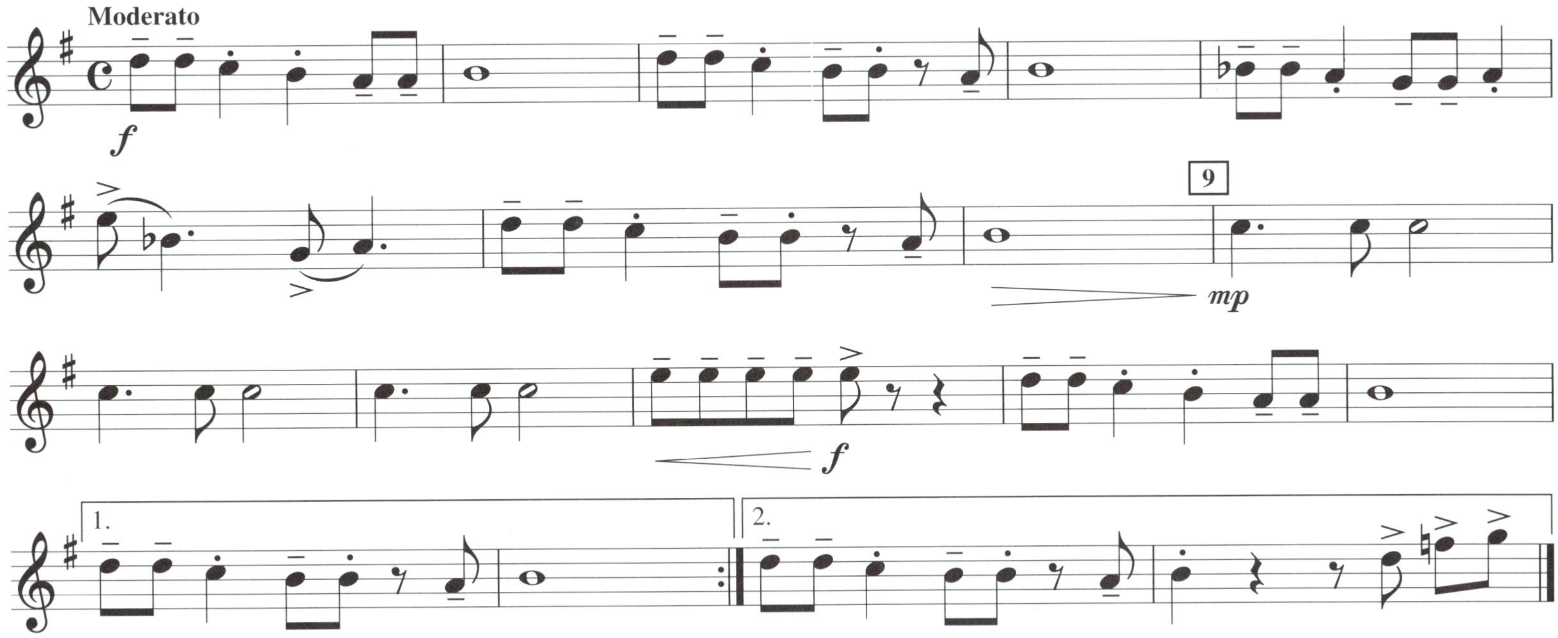

Moderato

f mp f

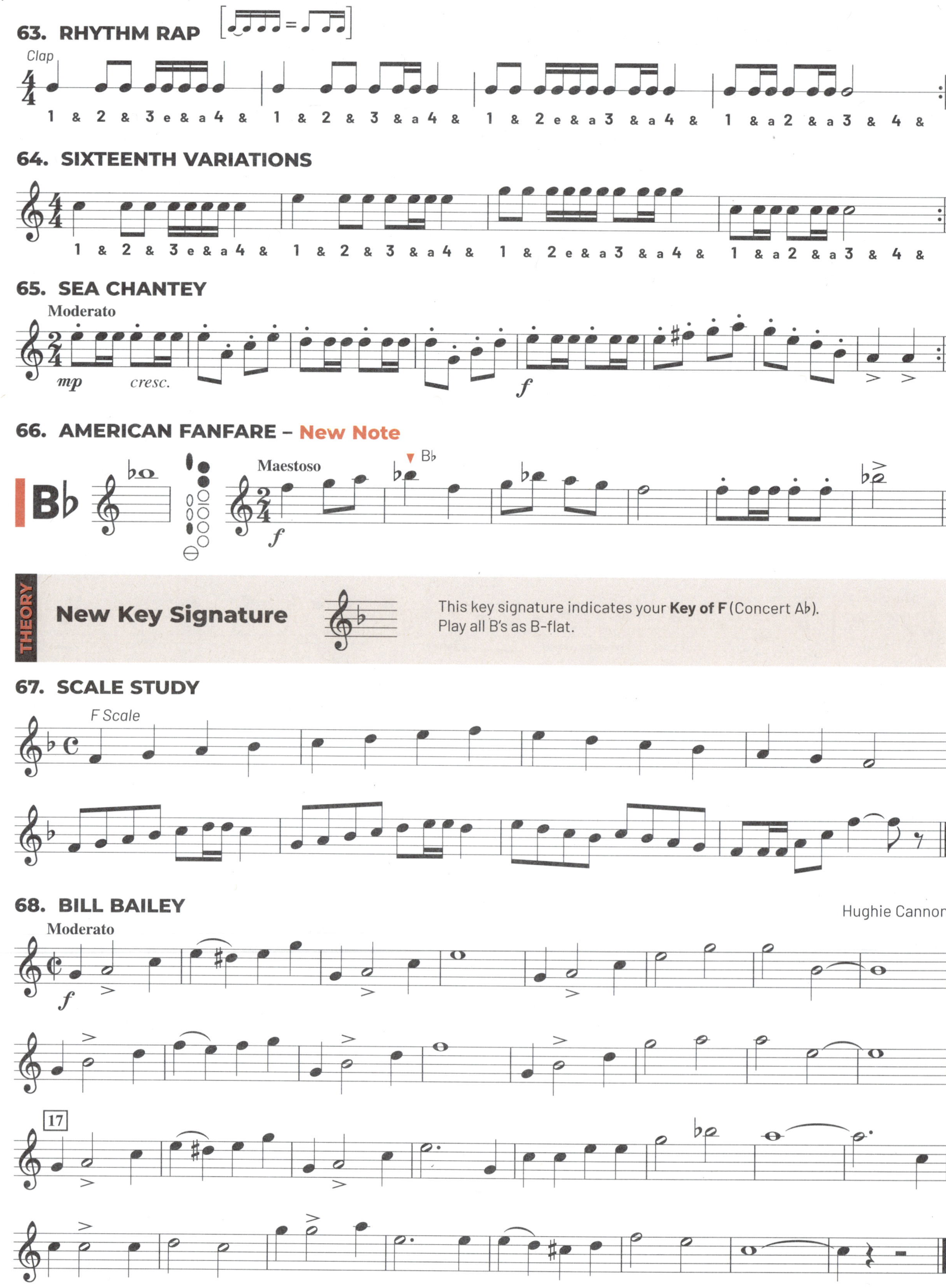
63. RHYTHM RAP
Clap
1 & 2 & 3 e & a 4 & 1 & 2 & 3 & a 4 & 1 & 2 e & a 3 & a 4 & 1 & a 2 & a 3 & 4 &
64. SIXTEENTH VARIATIONS
1 & 2 & 3 e & a 4 & 1 & 2 & 3 & a 4 & 1 & 2 e & a 3 & a 4 & 1 & a 2 & a 3 & 4 &
65. SEA CHANTEY
Moderato
mp
cresc.
f
66. AMERICAN FANFARE – New Note
B♭
Maestoso
B♭
f
THEORY
New Key Signature
This key signature indicates your Key of F (Concert A♭).
Play all B's as B-flat.
67. SCALE STUDY
F Scale
68. BILL BAILEY
Hughie Cannon
Moderato
f
17

69. RHYTHM RAP

70. RHYTHM ETUDE

71. BATTLE STATIONS

72. ENGLISH DANCE

73. BIG ROCK CANDY MOUNTAIN

American Folk Song

74. ESSENTIAL ELEMENTS QUIZ

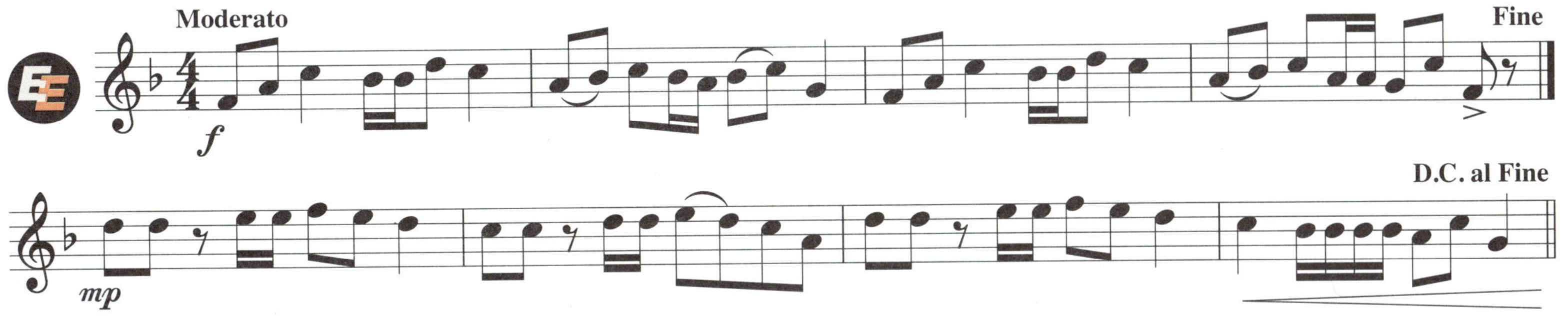

Looking for some more fun music to play?
See the inside front cover for instructions on accessing recent popular Bonus Songs.

Rallentando

rall. – Gradually slower (same as *ritardando*).

75. SIMPLE SONG – Duet

76. LINE DANCE

77. TECHNIQUE TRAX

78. THE GALWAY PIPER

79. MANHATTAN BEACH MARCH

John Philip Sousa

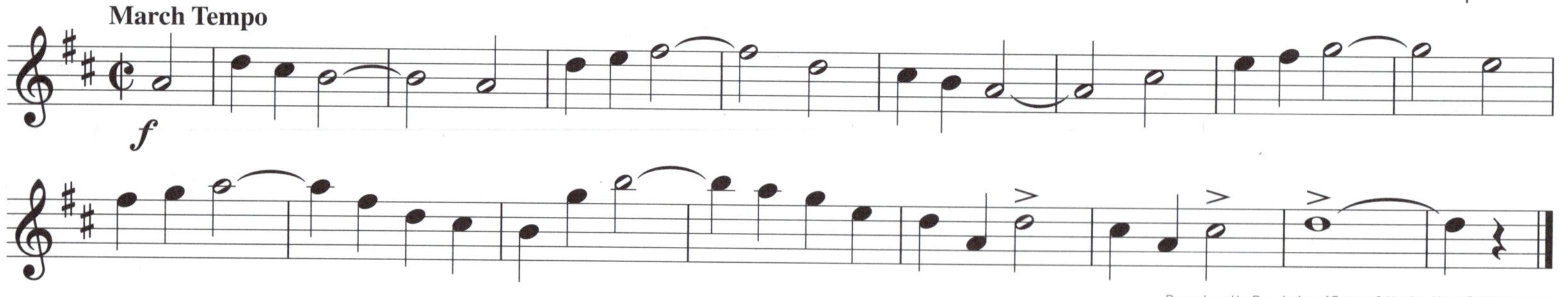

80. SIGHTREADING CHALLENGE

Remember the S-T-A-R-S guidelines.

81. RHYTHM RAP
Clap
1 e & a 2 & 3 & a 4 & 1 & a 2 & 3 & a 4 & 1 & a 2 & 3 & a 4 & 1 & a 2 & 3 & 4 &
82. MARCHING ALONG
1 e & a 2 & 3 & a 4 & 1 & a 2 & 3 & a 4 & 1 & a 2 & 3 & a 4 & 1 & a 2 & 3 & 4 &
83. FANFARE FOR BAND – Trio
Maestoso
A
B
C
f
84. O TANNENBAUM
German Carol
Andante
mp
1.
2.
mf
f
rall.
85. S'VIVON
Traditional Hanukkah Song
Moderato
mf
f
mp
f
mp
86. GOOD KING WENCESLAS
English Carol
Allegretto
mf
rit.

DAILY WARM-UPS

WORK-OUTS FOR TONE & TECHNIQUE

87. TONE BUILDER *Play at a very slow tempo.*

88. FLEXIBILITY STUDY

89. TECHNIQUE TRAX

90. CHORALE

Johann Sebastian Bach

HISTORY

French composer **Georges Bizet** (1838–1875) entered the Paris Conservatory to study music when he was only ten years old. There he won many awards for voice, piano, organ, and composition. Bizet's best known composition is the opera *Carmen*, which was first performed in 1875. *Carmen* tells the story of a band of Gypsies, soldiers, smugglers, and outlaws. Originally criticized for its realism on stage, it was soon hailed as the most popular French opera ever written.

91. TOREADOR SONG (from CARMEN)

Georges Bizet

92. LA CUMPARSITA – New Note (Enharmonic)

G. Rodriguez

93. THE YELLOW ROSE OF TEXAS *Check the key signature.*

American Folk Song

94. SCALE STUDY – New Note

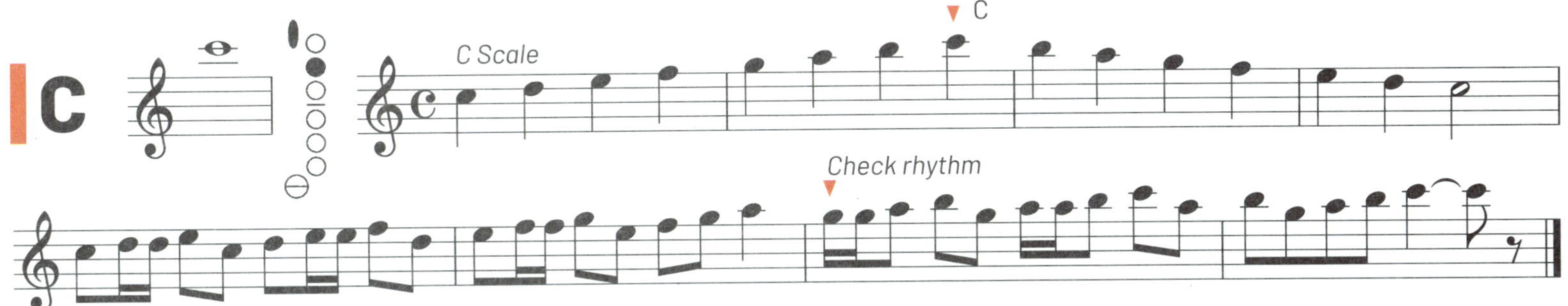

HISTORY

Until 1974 Australia's official national anthem was *God Save The Queen*. A competition was held in 1973 to compose a new anthem, but none of the entries met with the judges' approval. Finally the government asked the public to vote, choosing from among Australia's 3 most popular patriotic songs. After easily defeating *Waltzing Matilda* and *God Save The Queen*, *Advance Australia Fair* was officially declared the national anthem of Australia on April 19, 1974.

95. ADVANCE AUSTRALIA FAIR

Peter Dodds McCormick

96. ESSENTIAL CREATIVITY

Arrange the melody of "America (My Country 'Tis Of Thee)" for your instrument. Write out the first line (6 measures). Your first note is D. ADD: Key signature—key of D • Time signature—3/4 • Tempo and dynamic markings.

Play the completed line on your instrument to hear your own version.

97. AMERICAN PATROL

98. ARIA (from MARRIAGE OF FIGARO)

HISTORY

American composer **John Philip Sousa** (1854–1932) was best known for his brilliant band marches. Sousa wrote 136 marches, including *The Stars and Stripes Forever*, which was declared the official march of the United States of America in 1987.

99. THE STARS AND STRIPES FOREVER

John Philip Sousa

100. SIGHTREADING CHALLENGE *Remember the S-T-A-R-S guidelines.*

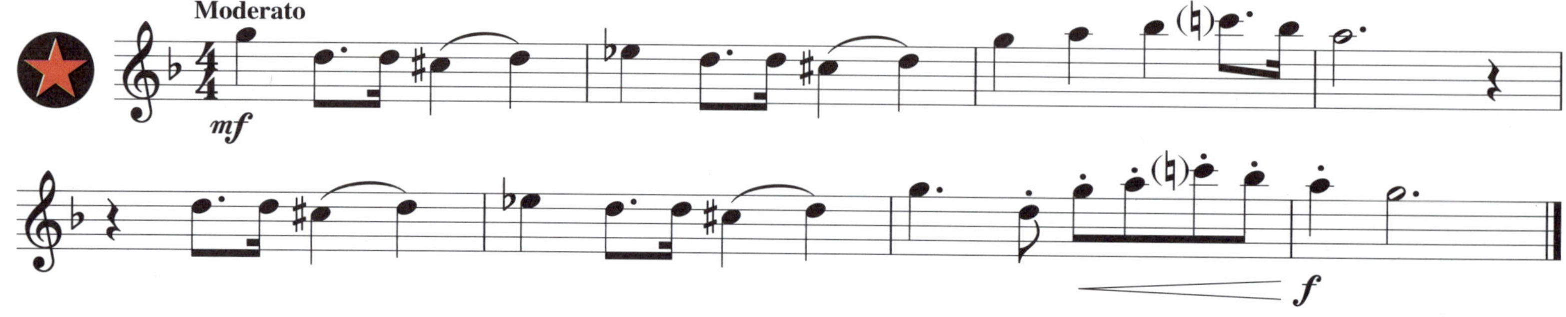

6/8 Time Signature

6/8 = **6 beats** per measure
= **Eighth** note gets one beat

♪ = 1 beat ♩ = 2 beats
♩. = 3 beats 𝅗𝅥. = 6 beats

THEORY

6/8 time is usually played with a slight emphasis on the **1st** and **4th** beats of each measure. This divides the measure into 2 groups of 3 beats each. In faster music, these two primary beats will make the music feel like it's counted "in 2."

101. RHYTHM RAP *Clap the rhythm while counting and tapping.*

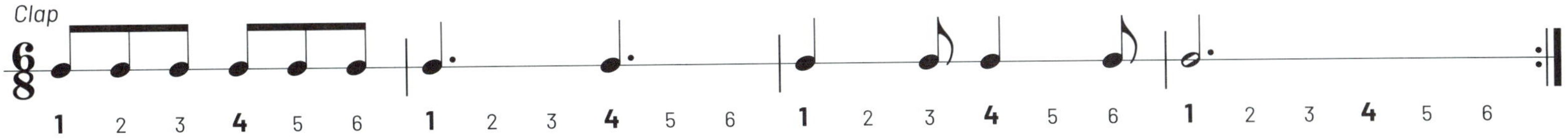
Clap
1 2 3 4 5 6 1 2 3 4 5 6 1 2 3 4 5 6 1 2 3 4 5 6

102. LAZY DAY

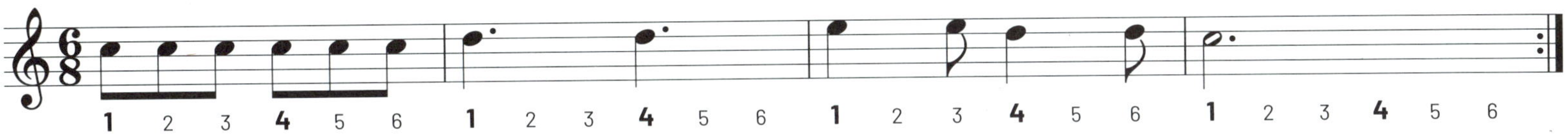
1 2 3 4 5 6 1 2 3 4 5 6 1 2 3 4 5 6 1 2 3 4 5 6

103. ROW YOUR BOAT

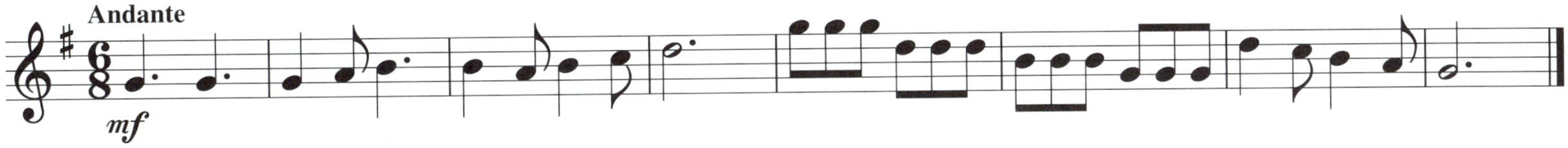
Andante
mf

104. JOLLY GOOD FELLOW

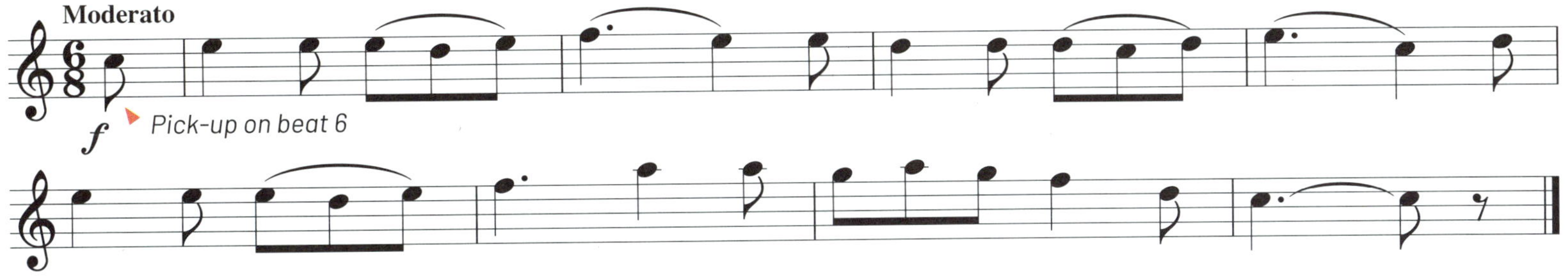
Moderato
f
Pick-up on beat 6

105. CHANSON

French Folk Song

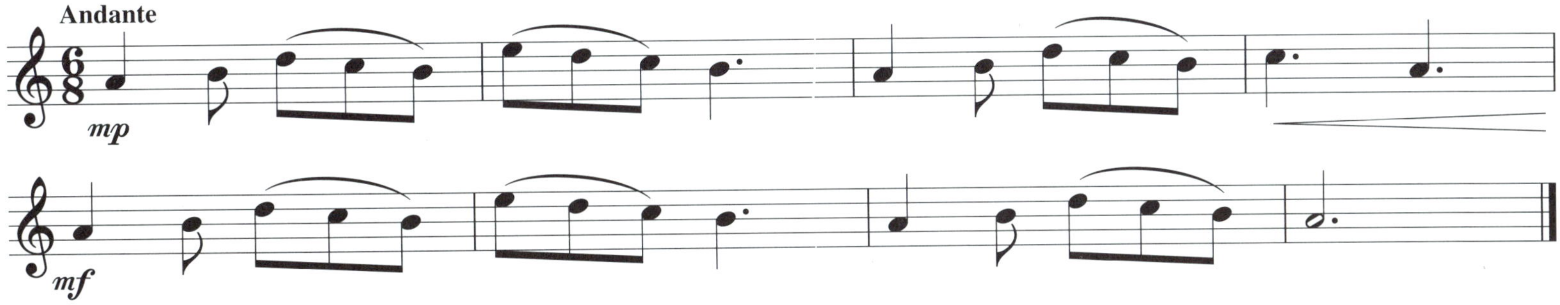
Andante
mp
mf

106. ESSENTIAL ELEMENTS QUIZ – WHEN JOHNNY COMES MARCHING HOME

American Folk Song

Allegro
mf
Count: 1 2 3 4 5 6
cresc.
f

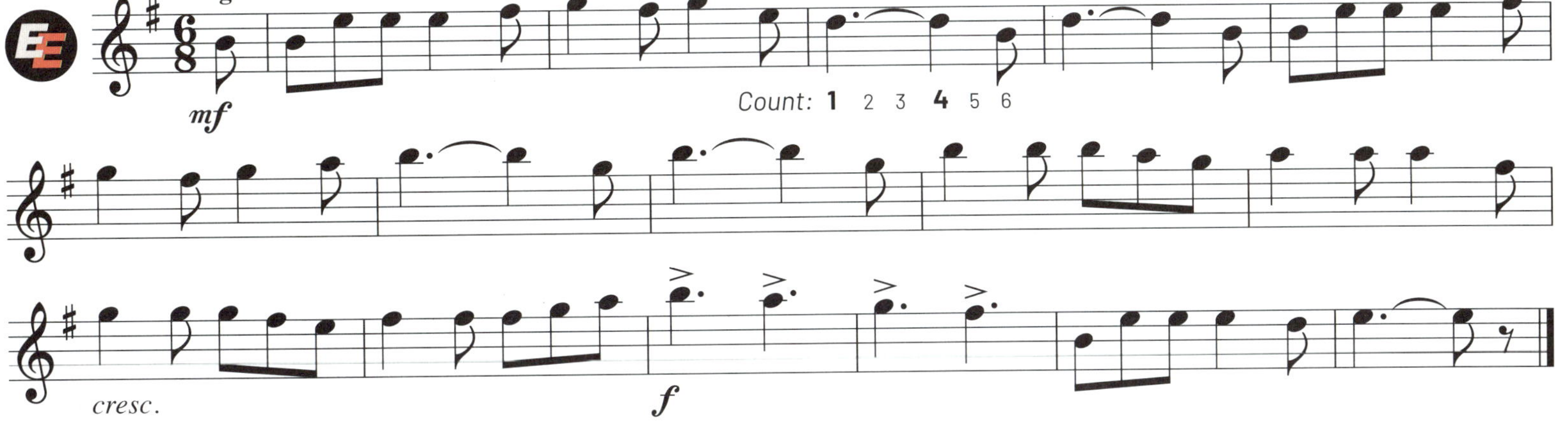

THEORY

More Enharmonics

Remember that notes which sound the same but have different letter names are called **enharmonics**. These are some common enharmonics that you'll use in the exercises below.

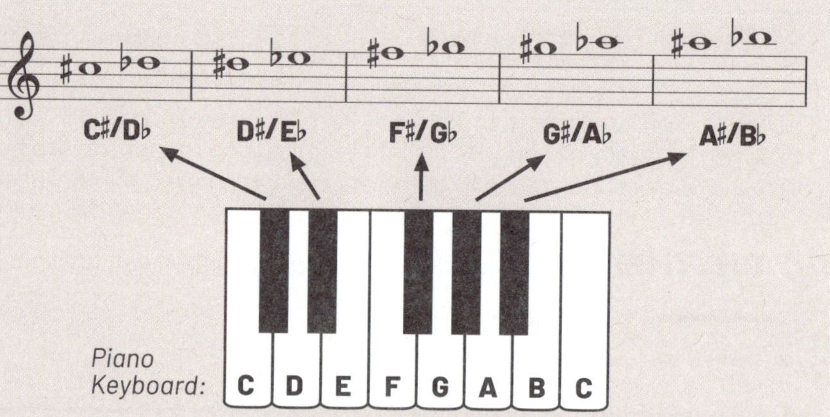

More Chromatics

The smallest distance between two notes is a half-step, and a scale made up of consecutive half-steps is a **chromatic scale**. These are usually written with **enharmonic** notes—sharps when going up and flats when going down.

Learn to use the suggested **alternate fingerings** for smoother technique in chromatic note combinations.

107. CHROMATIC SCALE *Practice slowly until you are sure of all the fingerings.*

108. TECHNIQUE TRAX

HISTORY

A **Habañera** is a Cuban dance and song form in slow 2/4 meter. It is named after the city of Havana, the capital of Cuba. Made popular in the New World in the early 19th Century, it was later carried over to Spain. There the rhythms of the Habañera were incorporated into many styles of Latin music. One of the most famous Habañeras is heard in Bizet's *Carmen*, written in 1875.

109. HABAÑERA (from CARMEN)

Georges Bizet

110. CHROMATIC CRESCENDO

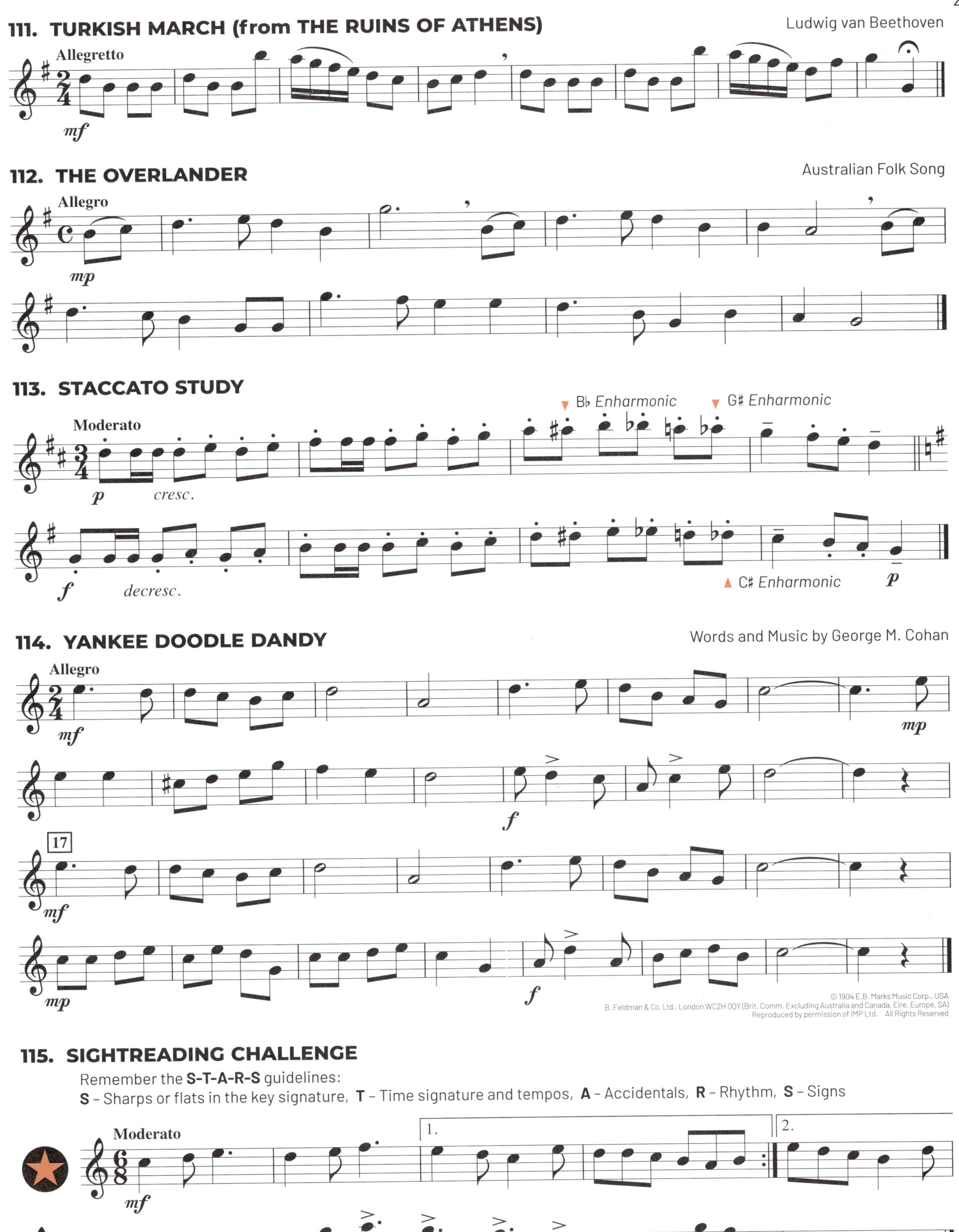
111. TURKISH MARCH (from THE RUINS OF ATHENS)
Ludwig van Beethoven
Allegretto
mf
112. THE OVERLANDER
Australian Folk Song
Allegro
mp
113. STACCATO STUDY
B♭ Enharmonic
G♯ Enharmonic
Moderato
p
cresc.
f
decresc.
C♯ Enharmonic
p
114. YANKEE DOODLE DANDY
Words and Music by George M. Cohan
Allegro
mf
mp
f
17
mf
mp
f
© 1904 E.B. Marks Music Corp., USA
B. Feldman & Co. Ltd., London WC2H 0QY (Brit. Comm. Excluding Australia and Canada, Eire, Europe, SA)
Reproduced by permission of IMP Ltd. All Rights Reserved
115. SIGHTREADING CHALLENGE
Remember the S-T-A-R-S guidelines:
S - Sharps or flats in the key signature, T - Time signature and tempos, A - Accidentals, R - Rhythm, S - Signs
Moderato
1.
2.
mf
f

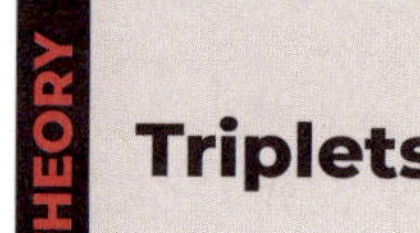

Triplets

A **triplet** is a group of **3** notes played in the space of **2**. In $\frac{2}{4}$, $\frac{3}{4}$, or $\frac{4}{4}$ time, an eighth note triplet is spread evenly across one beat.

116. RHYTHM RAP

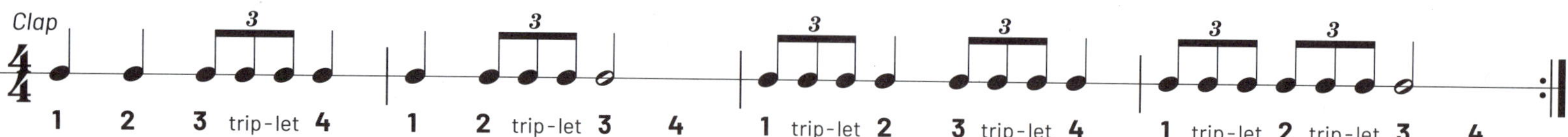

117. THREE TO GET READY

118. TRIPLET STUDY

119. MARCH (from THE NUTCRACKER) – Duet

Peter I. Tchaikovsky

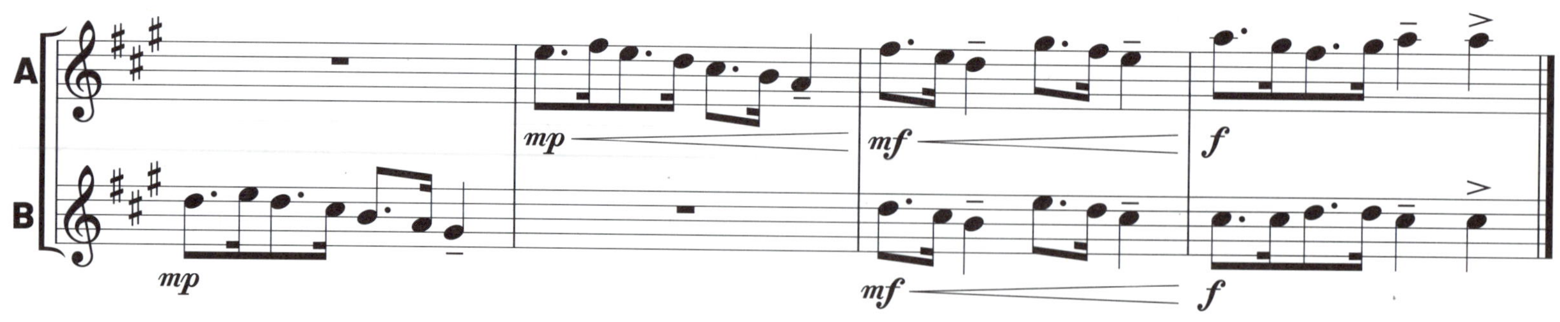

120. ESSENTIAL ELEMENTS QUIZ – THEME FROM FAUST

Charles Gounod

121. SCALE STUDY – New Notes

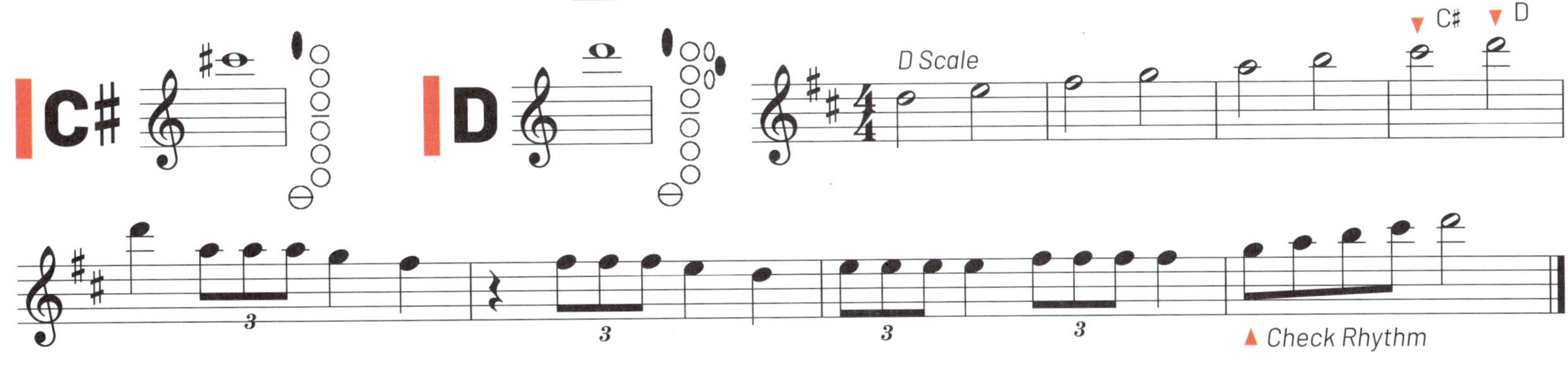

122. OVER THE RIVER AND THROUGH THE WOODS

123. RHYTHM RAP

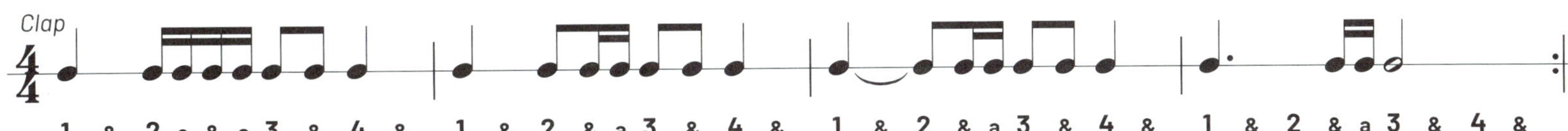

124. ON THE MOVE

125. HIGHER GROUND

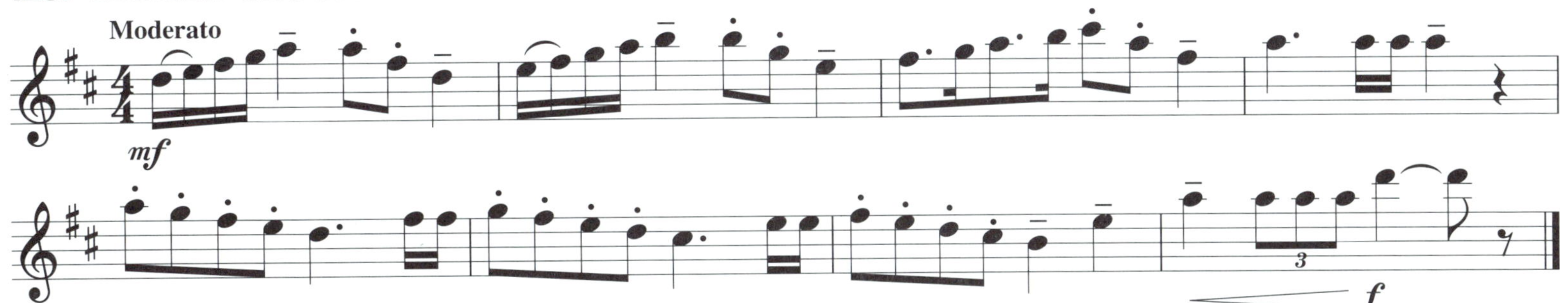

126. ESSENTIAL ELEMENTS QUIZ

HISTORY

The first known printing of the lyrics and music to **The Marines' Hymn** dates from August 1, 1918. An unknown author is believed to have taken the opening words of the song from the words on the Marine Corps flag, "From the halls of Montezuma to the shores of Tripoli." The music was taken from "Genevieve de Brabant," by the operetta composer Jacques Offenbach.

127. THE MARINES' HYMN

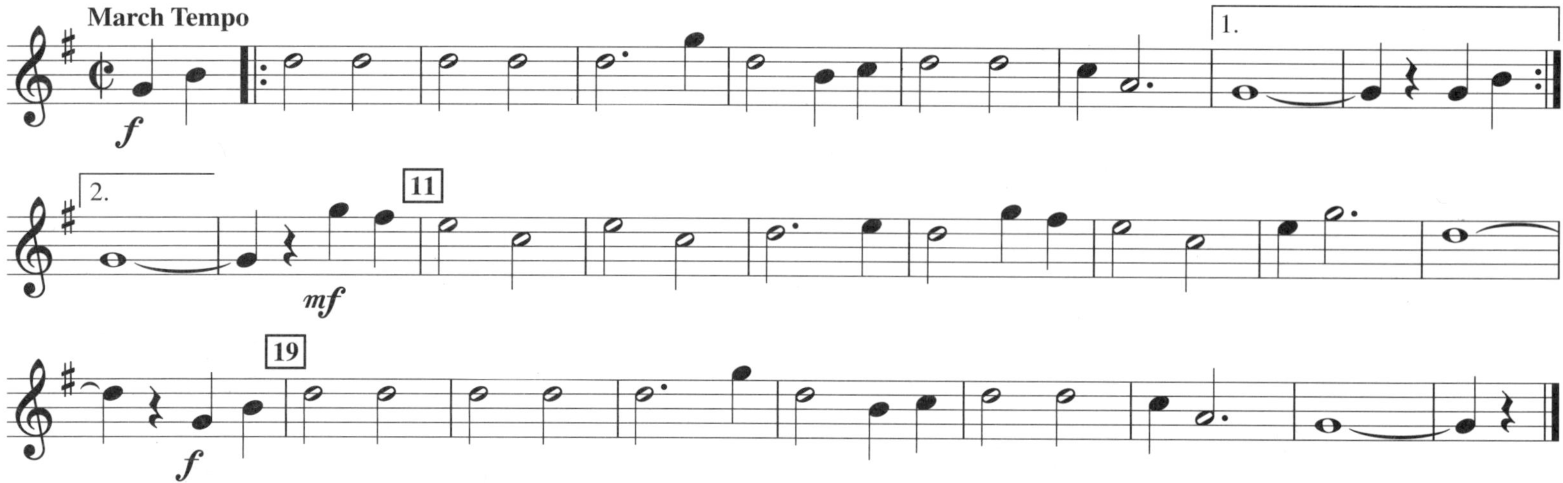

D.S. al Fine

Play until you see the **D.S. al Fine**. Then go back to the sign (𝄋) and play until the word **Fine**. **D.S.** is the abbreviation for **Dal Segno**, or "from the sign," and **Fine** means "the end."

128. D.S. MARCH

Accelerando

accel. – Gradually faster.

129. CAN-CAN

Jacques Offenbach

▲ *Watch your director.*

130. TARANTELLA

Italian Folk Song

The **waltz** is a dance in moderate 3/4 time which developed around 1800 from the Ländler, an Austrian peasant dance. Austrian composer **Johann Strauss, Jr.** (1825–1899) composed over 400 waltzes. These include such famous pieces as *The Blue Danube*, *Tales From the Vienna Woods* and *Emperor Waltz*.

HISTORY

131. EMPEROR WALTZ

Johann Strauss, Jr.

Legato Style

legato – Played in a smooth, connected style.

132. ENGLISH DANCE – Duet

Johann Christian Bach

133. ESSENTIAL ELEMENTS QUIZ – BRITISH GRENADIERS

Traditional

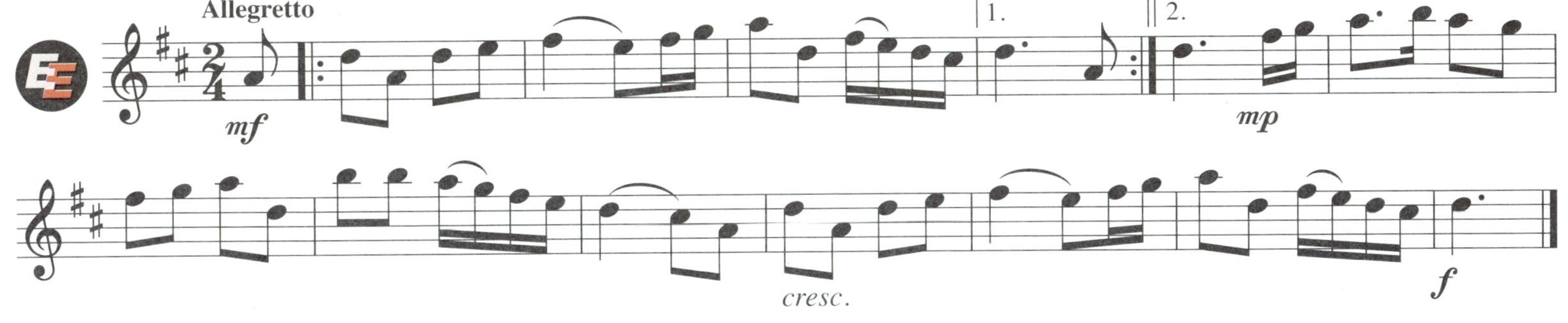

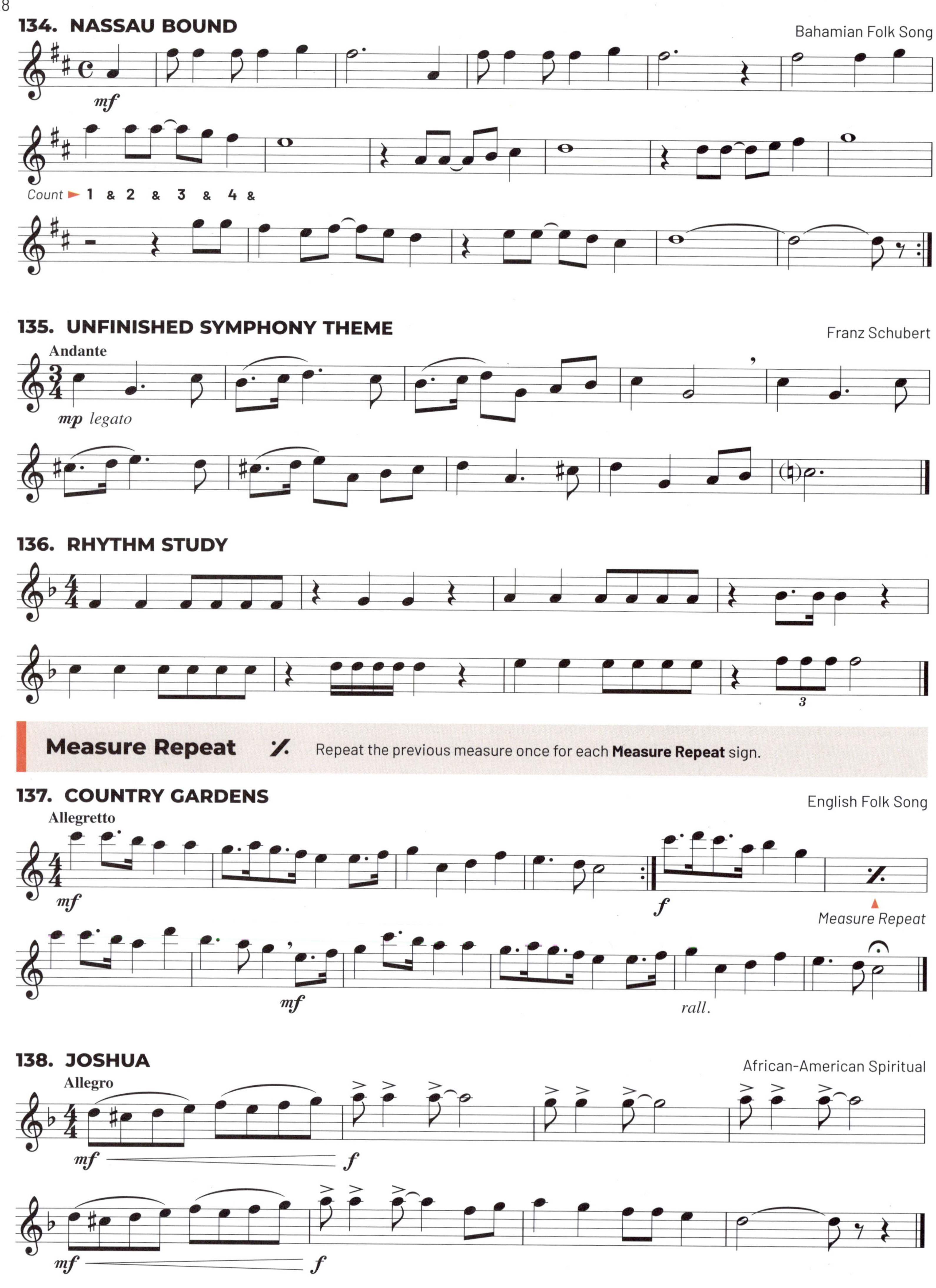
134. NASSAU BOUND
Bahamian Folk Song
mf
Count 1 & 2 & 3 & 4 &
135. UNFINISHED SYMPHONY THEME
Franz Schubert
Andante
mp legato
136. RHYTHM STUDY
3
Measure Repeat
Repeat the previous measure once for each Measure Repeat sign.
137. COUNTRY GARDENS
English Folk Song
Allegretto
mf
f
Measure Repeat
mf
rall.
138. JOSHUA
African-American Spiritual
Allegro
mf
f
mf
f

139. LISTEN TO THE MOCKINGBIRD
Alice Hawthorne
Moderato
mf
Pick-up
140. ANCHORS AWEIGH
Capt. A.H. Miles and C.A. Zimmerman
March Tempo
f
mf
cresc.
1.
2.
f
f
141. GREENSLEEVES
English Folk Song
Andante
p
mf
rit.
142. THE LONG CLIMB
Measure Repeat
143. THE BLUE BELLS OF SCOTLAND
Scottish Folk Song
Moderato
f
1.
2.
mf
f

Major and Minor

The scales you've already learned are called **Major** scales. They all follow the same pattern, with **half-steps** between notes 3–4 and between notes 7–8.

Natural Minor scales follow a different pattern, with **half-steps** between notes 2–3 and 5–6. The **E Minor** scale uses the same key signature as **G Major**.

Another type of minor scale is called **Harmonic Minor**, which adds an accidental to raise the **7th** note by a half-step. Compare the scales on the right.

See page 37 for additional minor scales.

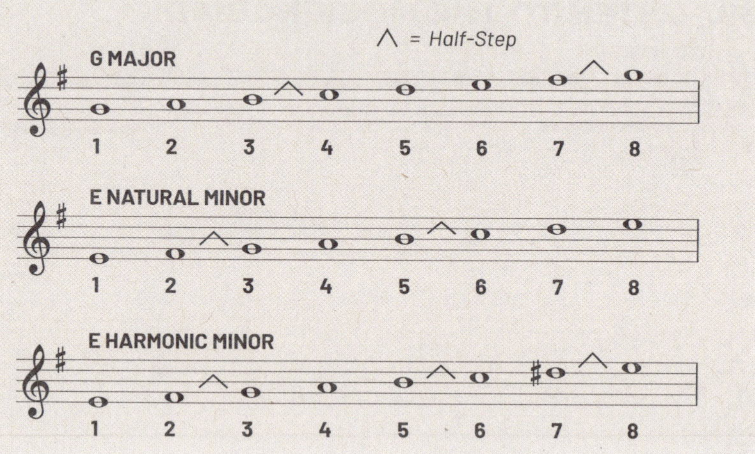

144. NATURAL MINOR SCALE

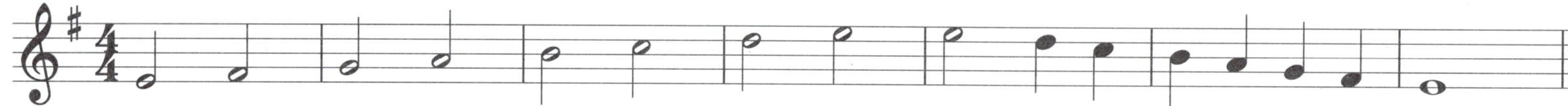

145. FINALE FROM "NEW WORLD SYMPHONY"

Antonin Dvorák

146. HARMONIC MINOR SCALE

147. HUNGARIAN DANCE NO. 5

Johannes Brahms

148. POMP AND CIRCUMSTANCE (LAND OF HOPE AND GLORY)

Edward Elgar

PERFORMANCE SPOTLIGHT

D.S. al Coda Play until you see the **D.S. al Coda**. Then go back to the sign (𝄋) and play until the **Coda Sign** ("To Coda" 𝄌). Skip directly to the **Coda** and play until the end.

149. SIMPLE GIFTS – Band Arrangement

Shaker Folk Song
Arr. by John Higgins

150. SEMPER FIDELIS – Band Arrangement

John Philip Sousa
Arr. by John Higgins

Additional Bonus Songs are available online. See the inside front cover for details.

PERFORMANCE SPOTLIGHT

153. SERENGETI (AFRICAN RHAPSODY) – Band Arrangement

John Higgins

Maestoso "Daybreak"
f
mp
rit.
5 Forceful
f
3
9 "Safari"
mf
19
27
mp
sim.
37
f
decresc.
mp rit.
45 Moderately Fast
4
49 "Celebration"
Play 3 times
Play 2nd & 3rd time only
mf – f
Play all times
mf
57
mf
mp
rit.
65 "Sunset"
Slowly
3
p

RUBANK® STUDIES

154. CHORALE

p cresc. — *mf decresc.* — *p*

155. CHORALE

mp — *mf* — *mp*

156. CHORALE

p — *mp* — *p* — *mp* — *p*

157. CHORALE

mp — *mf* — *mp*

158. CHORALE

p — *mp* — *p*

ALTO SAXOPHONE KEY OF G (CONCERT B♭)

159.

RUBANK® STUDIES

ALTO SAXOPHONE KEY OF C (CONCERT E♭)

163.

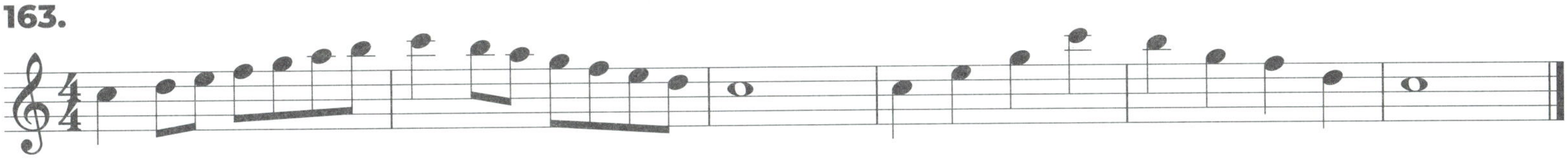

164.

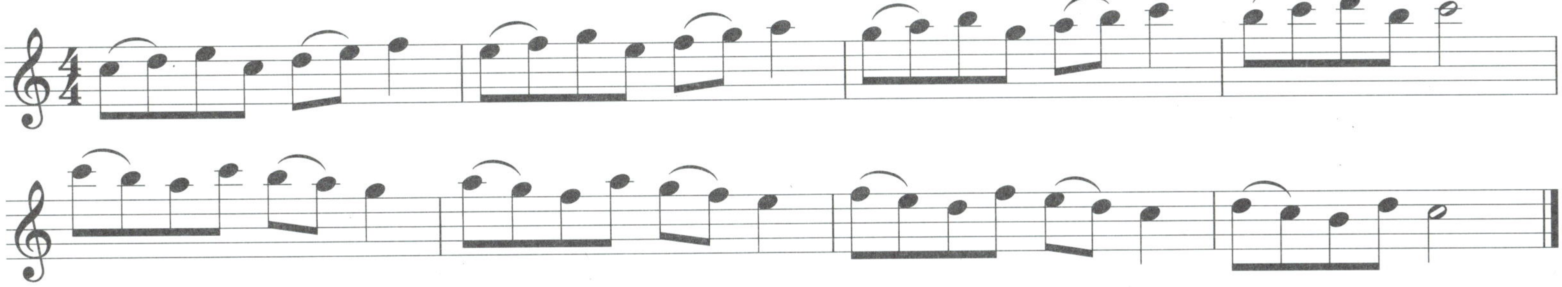

165.

166.

ALTO SAXOPHONE KEY OF D (CONCERT F)

167.

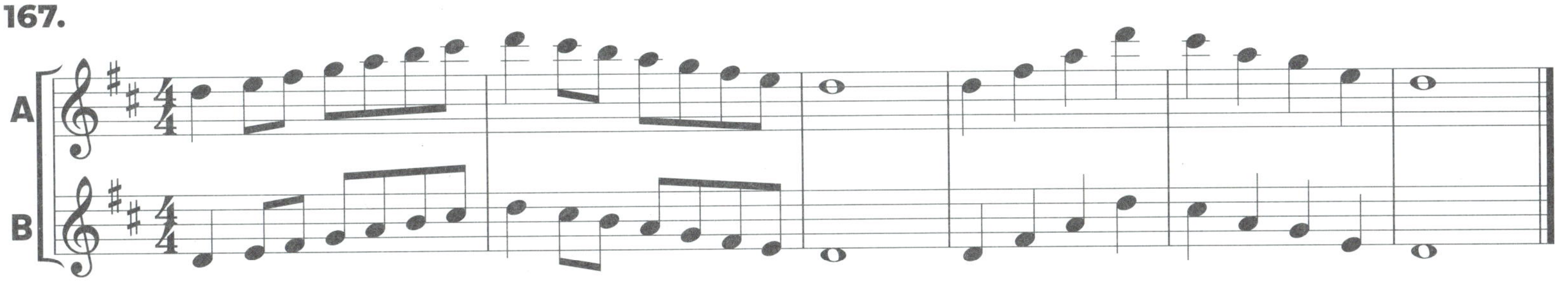

A

B

168.

169.

170.

Alt. Alt.

RUBANK® STUDIES

ALTO SAXOPHONE KEY OF F (CONCERT A♭)

171.

172.

173.

174.

ALTO SAXOPHONE KEY OF A (CONCERT C)

175.

176.

177.

178.

RUBANK® STUDIES

ALTO SAXOPHONE KEY OF E MINOR (CONCERT G MINOR)

ALTO SAXOPHONE KEY OF A MINOR (CONCERT C MINOR)

ALTO SAXOPHONE KEY OF B MINOR (CONCERT D MINOR)

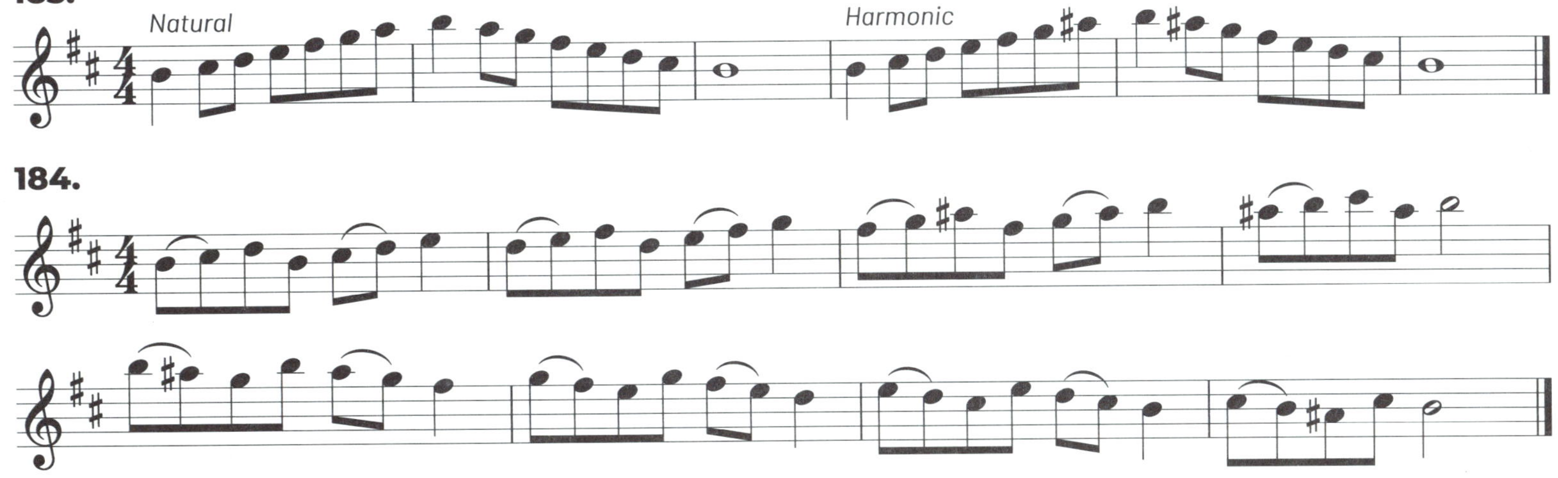

CHROMATIC SCALES

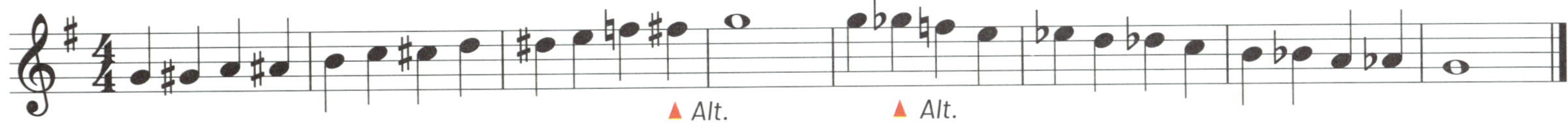

186.

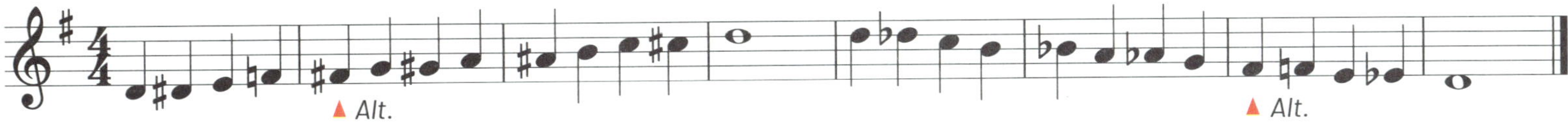

INDIVIDUAL STUDY – Alto Saxophone

187. BREATH CONTROL STUDY *Try both two and four measure phrases.*

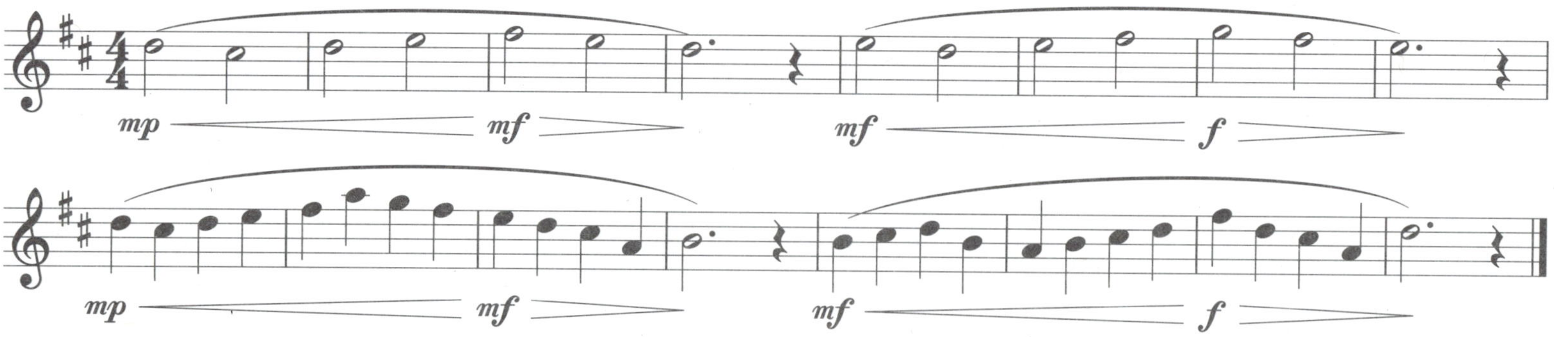

mp mf mf f

mp mf mf f

188. A♭ CONCERT ETUDE

189. ARTICULATION ETUDE

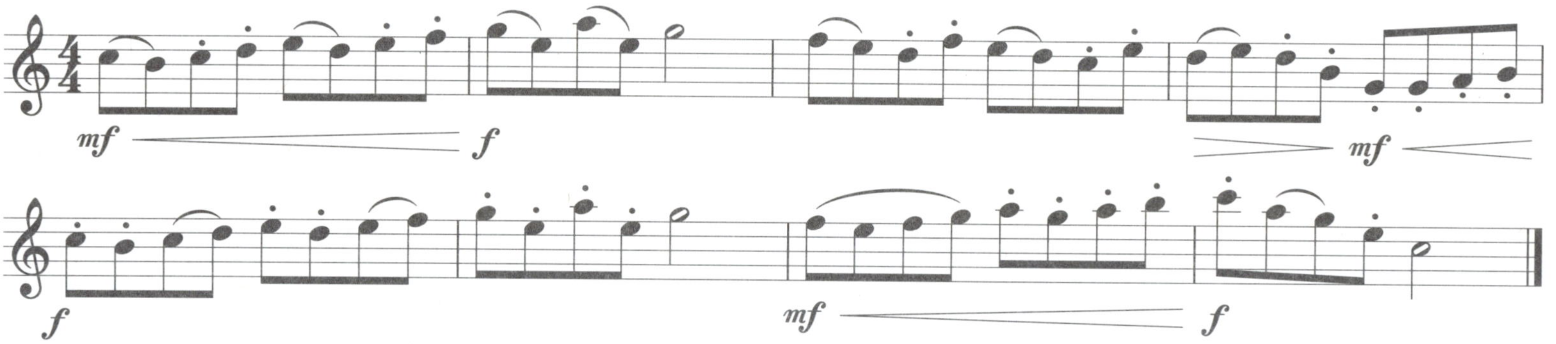

mf f mf

f mf f

190. ARPEGGIO STUDY

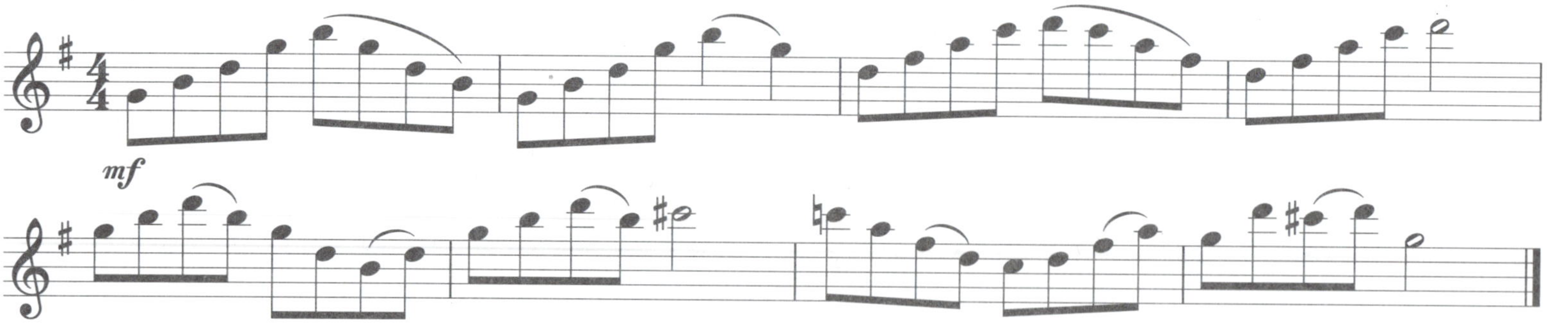

mf

191. TECHNIQUE CHALLENGE

Fine

D.C. al Fine

INDIVIDUAL STUDY – Alto Saxophone

INDIVIDUAL STUDY – Alto Saxophone

Solo with Piano Accompaniment

You can perform this solo with the piano accompaniment on the following page.

198. SONATINA from "Divertimento #2" – Alto Saxophone Solo

Online audio - see inside front cover to access.

Wolfgang Amadeus Mozart
Arr. by H. Voxman

Allegro (♩ = 104)

Piano *f*

3 *Play*

f

7

p

14

f *p* *f*

p 22 *f*

p

28

f

p *f* *rit.*

INDIVIDUAL STUDY – Alto Saxophone

198. SONATINA from "Divertimento #2" – Piano Accompaniment

Online audio – see inside front cover to access.

Wolfgang Amadeus Mozart
Arr. by H. Voxman

RHYTHM STUDIES

RHYTHM STUDIES

CREATING MUSIC

THEORY

Theme and Variation

Theme and Variation is a technique used by composers and arrangers to create interesting musical ideas that are "varied" from an established melody, or "theme." Play the following theme and two variations to hear how the arranger has created new phrases based on the original melody.

1. THEME

"Simple Gifts"

2. THEME AND YOUR VARIATION

Write your own variation of this theme. Use your instrument to hear and try different ideas.

"Candy Mountain Rock"

Theme

Your Variation

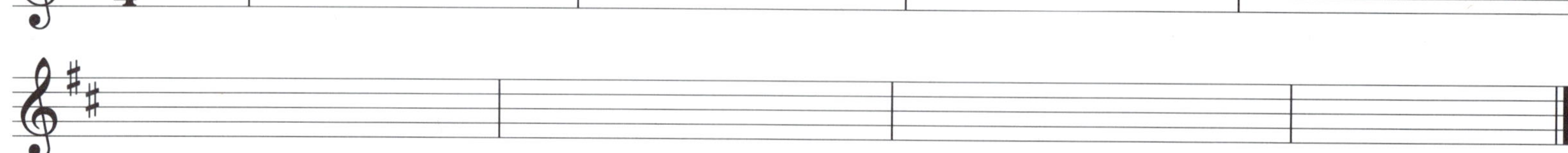

THEORY

Blues Improvisation

Improvisation using a **Blues Scale** is an important part of jazz and popular music. Musicians use combinations of these notes and various rhythms to create their own spontaneous solos over a 12 measure progression of chords.

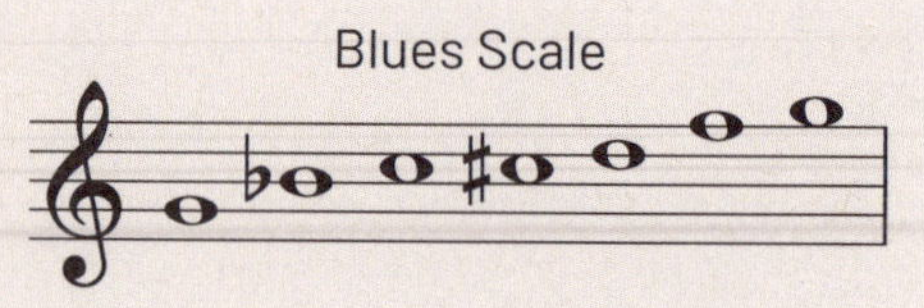

3. LET'S JAM

Use the indicated notes from the Blues Scale to create your own solo to play with the accompaniment (Line B).

You can mark your progress through the book on this page.
Fill in the stars as instructed by your band director.

1. Page 2-4, Review
2. Page 5, Sightreading Challenge, No. 19
3. Page 6, Daily Warm-Ups
4. Page 7, Sightreading Challenge, No. 31
5. Page 8, Essential Creativity, No. 38
6. Page 9, EE Quiz, No. 43
7. Page 10, Sightreading Challenge, No. 49
8. Page 11, EE Quiz, No. 55
9. Page 12-13, Performance Spotlight
10. Page 15, EE Quiz, No. 74
11. Page 16, Sightreading Challenge, No. 80
12. Page 18, Daily Warm-Ups
13. Page 19, Essential Creativity, No. 96
14. Page 20, Sightreading Challenge, No. 100
15. Page 21, EE Quiz, No. 106
16. Page 22, Chromatic Scale, No. 107
17. Page 23, Sightreading Challenge, No. 115
18. Page 24, EE Quiz, No. 120
19. Page 25, EE Quiz, No. 126
20. Page 27, EE Quiz, No. 133
21. Page 30, Natural Minor Scale, No. 144
22. Page 30, Harmonic Minor Scale, No. 146
23. Page 30, Pomp and Circumstance, No. 148
24. Page 31, Performance Spotlight
25. Page 32, Performance Spotlight
26. Page 33, Performance Spotlight
27. Page 38-39, Individual Study
28. Page 40, Performance Spotlight

MUSIC — AN ESSENTIAL ELEMENT OF LIFE

FINGERING CHART

E♭ ALTO SAXOPHONE

Instrument Care Reminders

Before putting your instrument back in its case after playing, do the following:

- Remove the reed, wipe off excess moisture and return it to the reed case.
- Remove the mouthpiece and wipe the inside with a clean cloth. Once a week, wash the mouthpiece with warm tap water. Dry thoroughly.
- Loosen the neck screw and remove the neck. Shake out excess moisture and dry the neck with a neck cleaner.
- Drop the weight of a chamois or cotton swab into the bell. Pull the swab through the body several times. Return the instrument to its case.
- Your case is designed to hold only specific objects. If you try to force anything else into the case, it may damage your instrument.

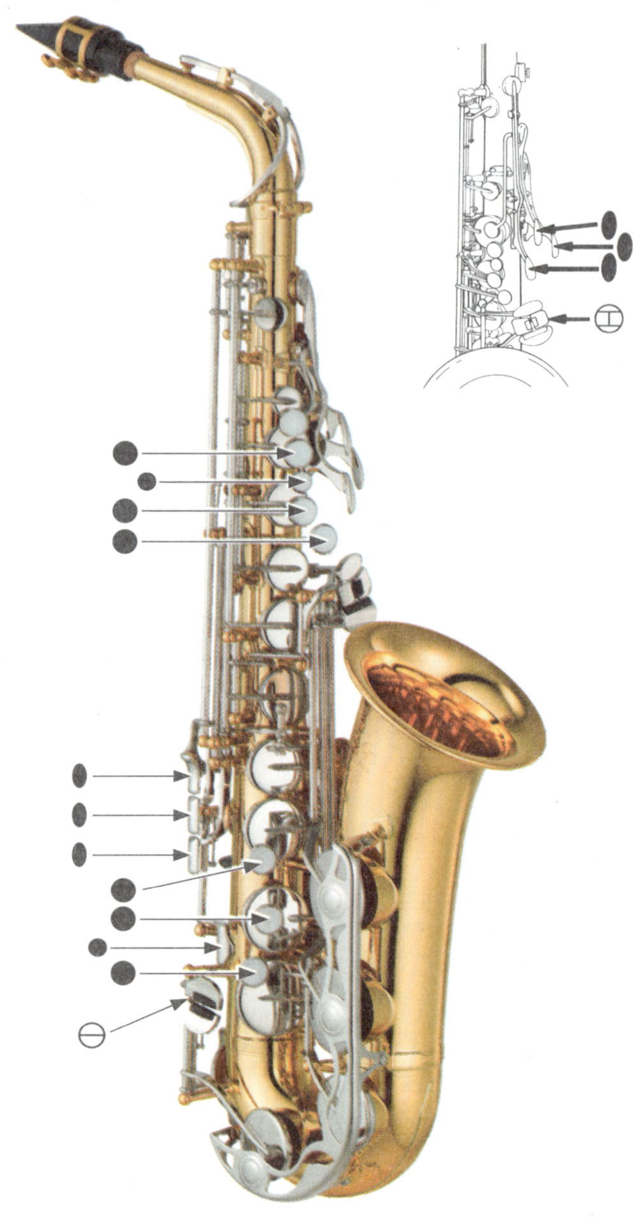

○ = Open

● = Pressed down

The most common fingering appears first when two fingerings are shown.

Instruments and photos courtesy of Yamaha.

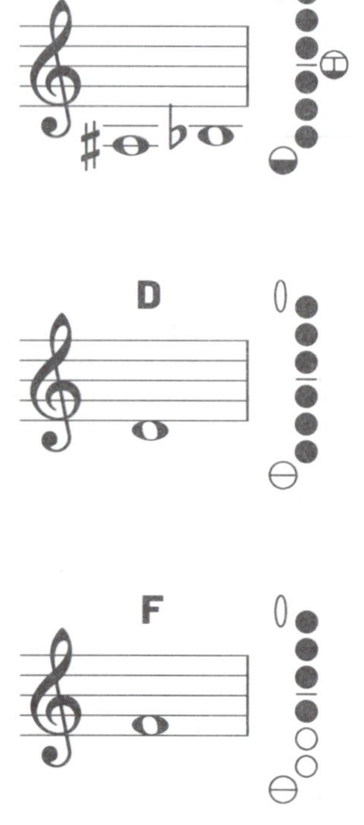

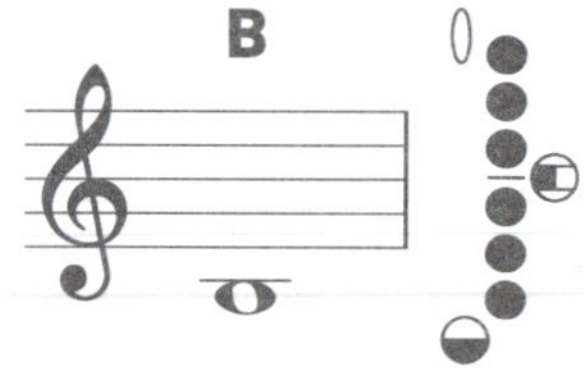

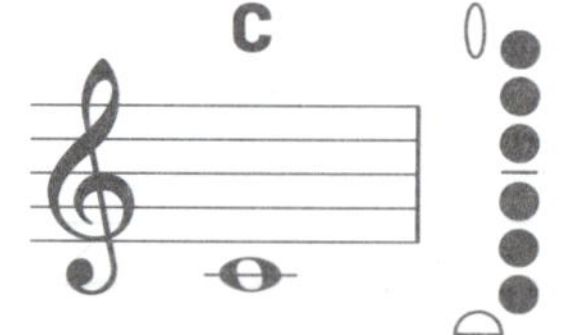

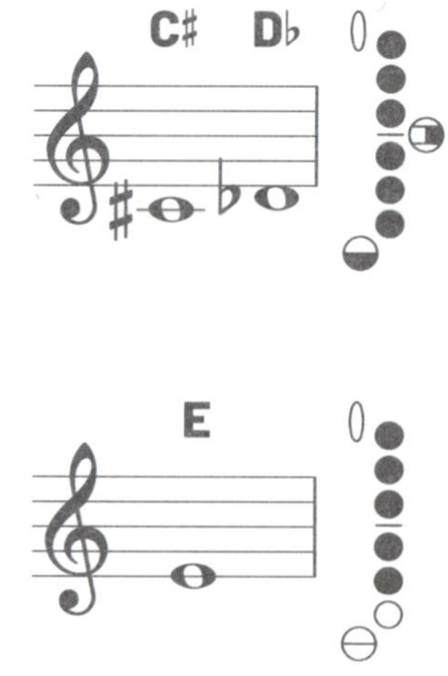

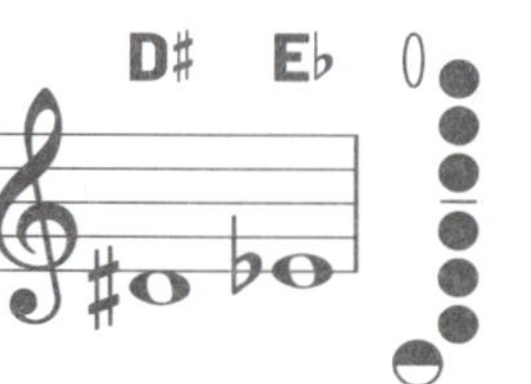

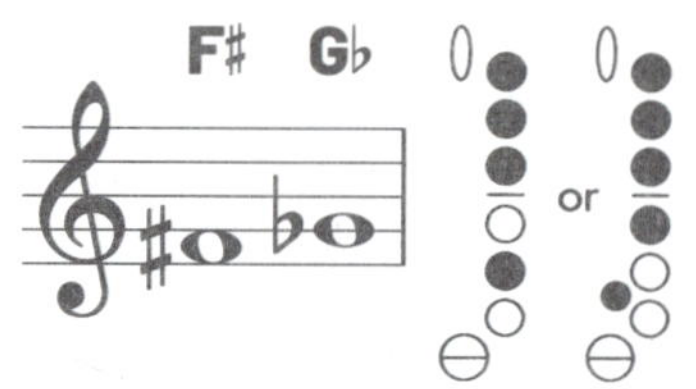

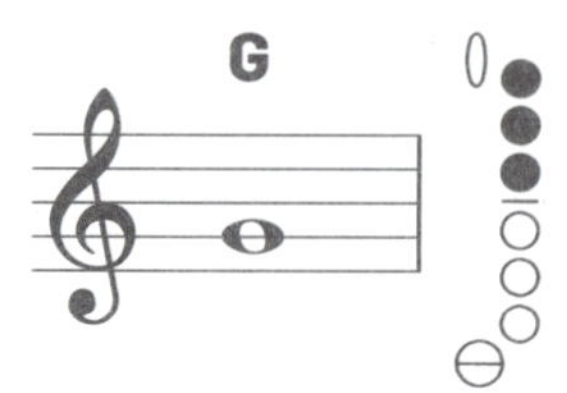

FINGERING CHART

E♭ ALTO SAXOPHONE

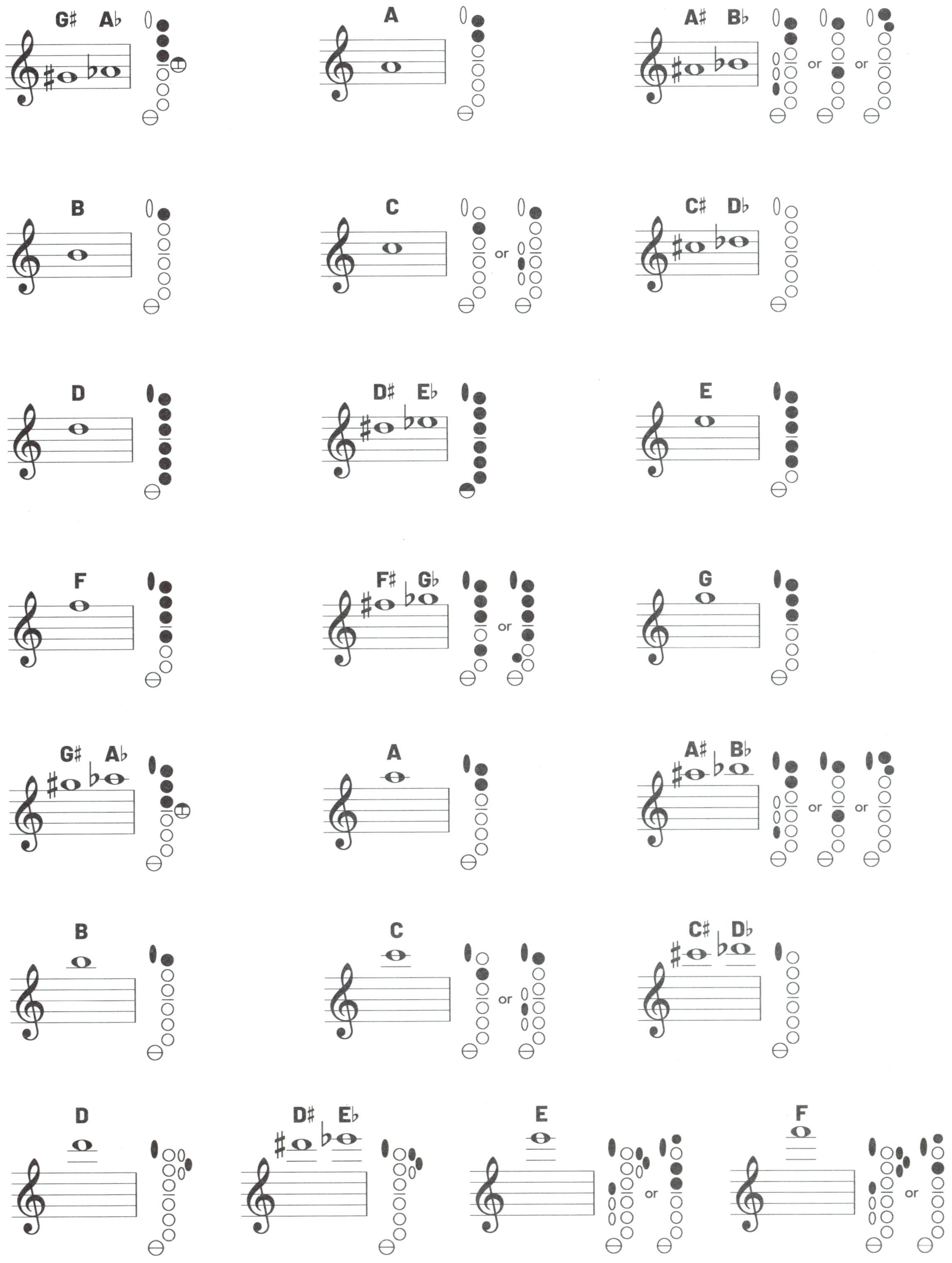

G♯ A♭

A

A♯ B♭ or or

B

C or

C♯ D♭

D

D♯ E♭

E

F

F♯ G♭ or

G

G♯ A♭

A

A♯ B♭ or or

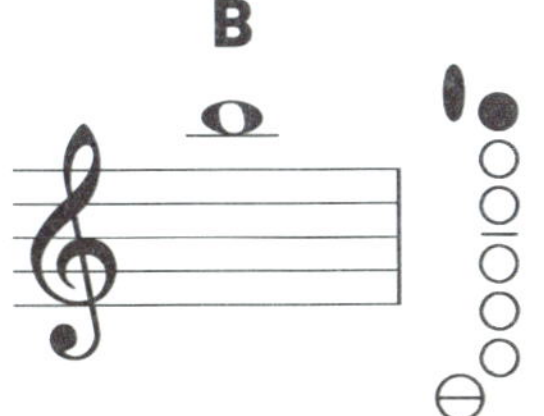

C or

C♯ D♭

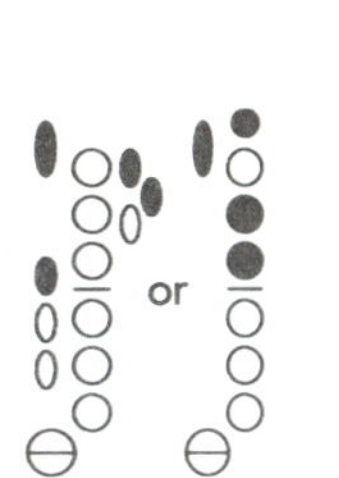

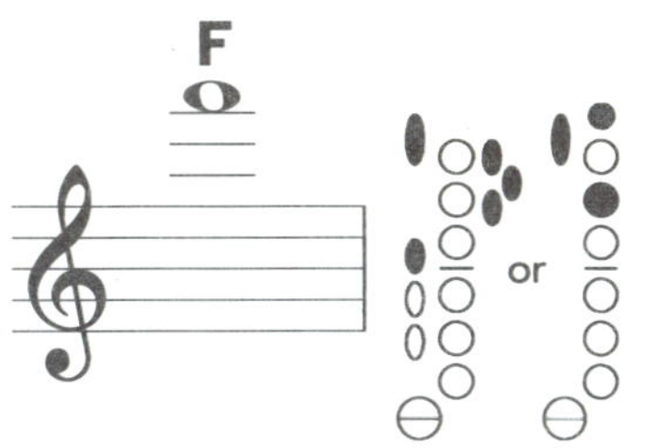

Reference Index

Definitions (pg.)

Book 1 Review

Composers

World Music